Ralph

24

The History and Culture of Ancient and Modern Egypt

By M. Clement Hall and Charles River Editors

About M. Clement Hall

AFGHAN INTERIM GOVERNMENT

Public Health Ministry

The Health Ministry of the Afghan Interim Government wishes to show its appreciation to MICHAEL HALL M.D. for contribution of Medical Aid to the Afghan people in their time of greatest need.

Dr. Najibullah Mujaddidi
First Deputy Minister of
Public Health, AIG.

After service in the ranks of the British Special Air Service (SAS) Regiment, M. Clement Hall became a physician and then an orthopaedic surgeon. He has held professorial positions in Canada, Vietnam and the United States, practicing and teaching orthopaedic surgery in three continents and during several wars. Somewhere along the way, time was found to operate a four hundred acre mixed farm, a one hundred seat restaurant and to obtain a licence as a flying instructor.

Hall's time spent in the service and in the Middle East has provided extensive knowledge and a unique perspective of Egypt and the Middle East.

About Charles River Editors

Charles River Editors was founded by Harvard and MIT alumni to provide superior editing and original writing services, with the expertise to create digital content for publishers across a vast range of subject matter. In addition to providing original digital content for third party publishers, Charles River Editors republishes civilization's greatest literary works, bringing them to a new generation via ebooks.

Visit charlesrivereditors.com for more information.

Introduction

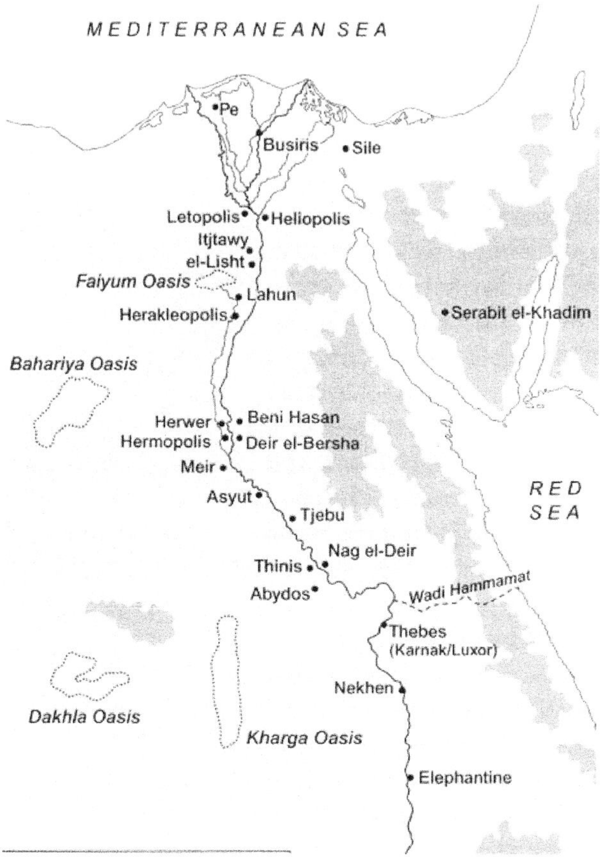

Ancient Egypt

Africa may have given rise to the first human beings, and Egypt probably gave rise to the first great civilizations, which continue to fascinate modern societies across the globe nearly 5,000 years later. From the Library and Lighthouse of Alexandria to the Great Pyramid at Giza, the Ancient Egyptians produced several wonders of the world, revolutionized architecture and construction, created some of the world's first systems of mathematics and medicine, and established language and art that spread across the known world. With world-famous leaders like King Tut and Cleopatra, it's no wonder that today's world has so many Egyptologists.

What makes the accomplishments of the Ancient Egyptians all the more remarkable is that Egypt was historically a place of great political turbulence. Its position made it both valuable and vulnerable to tribes across the Mediterranean and the Middle East, and Ancient Egypt had no shortage of its own internecine warfare. Its most famous conquerors would come from Europe, with Alexander the Great laying the groundwork for the Hellenic Ptolemy line and the Romans extinguishing that line after defeating Cleopatra and driving her to suicide.

The History and Culture of Ancient and Modern Egypt comprehensively covers the history and culture of Ancient Egypt, looking at its religious, political, foreign and military past, and examining all the architectural and artistic achievements from 3,000-30 B.C. Along with historic artwork depicting important people, places, and events, *The History of Ancient and Modern Egypt* will bring readers up to speed on Ancient Egypt today.

Modern Egypt

In the last year, Egypt has undergone a revolution that expelled its authoritarian leader of nearly 30 years and implemented elections that have pitted the Egyptian military in a power struggle with the Muslim Brotherhood, the long-time Islamic opposition group with ties to Hamas and elements of al-Qaeda. Making everything that much more surreal, the events have played out before well placed television cameras with continuous "real time" coverage of the revolution and ongoing turmoil, and foreign nations around the world eagerly await or dread the end result.

The situation in Egypt sounds messy today, but strife in Egypt is hardly a new occurrence. In fact, conflict has been more of a rule than exception since the end of the 18th century, when Western powers, beginning with Napoleon and the French, got involved in the territory that was at that point a part of the Ottoman Turkish Empire. Since then, European powers came into conflict with each other and local Egyptian officials in their imperialistic efforts, Egyptian nationalists tried to do away with foreign interference, and the critically important Suez Canal became a geopolitical hotspot. And when Egypt finally did receive full independence and sovereignty from the British, it was subjected to conflict between religious extremists, secular forces, pan-Arab nationalists, and oppressive strongmen.

The History and Culture of Ancient and Modern Egypt comprehensively covers this turbulent history, helping to explain and sort through all the different forces at play in Egypt over the last 215 years. At the same time, it examines and analyzes all of the different religious, political, foreign, and military issues that continue to affect Egypt today. *The History of Modern Egypt* will bring readers up to speed on one of the world's crucial countries today.

Ancient Egypt

Overview

Egypt is the Nile and the Nile is Egypt. Geophysically and spiritually Egypt represents the contrast between life and death.

Death was the desert, named the Red Land by the ancient inhabitants of Egypt, with the word *Deshret* from which we derive our own word "desert." Incidentally, deshret also represented the crown of Lower Egypt.

Deshret, the Crown of Lower Egypt

Life was the Black Land, the loam that was swept down with the miraculous annual filling of the Nile, despite the minimal rainfall in Egypt itself. And death by starvation was to be expected if the annual flooding of the Nile were to fail.

On this one issue is built Egypt's theocracy and history – the preservation of a people by irrigation of the land.

Our knowledge of the early history of Egypt is based in part on interpretation of excavations and in part on "King Lists," as left to posterity by an Egyptian priest, Manetho, who lived during the Ptolemaic Era of Egypt (305 – 30 B.C.). Inevitably every issue is open to argument and reading the texts can be made tedious by the academic requirement – "although Professor Smith claims this, Herr Doktor Schmidt has disproved that, and Professeur Dupont asserts they are both wrong." So, the artifacts are real, the exact interpretation of their meaning, and their exact dating remains open to endless argument. In this work we follow the dates given by the *Oxford History of Ancient Egypt*

Egyptologists are fortunate in the wealth of material available to them. The dry climate preserved the physical structures in the most remarkable manner, both the structures made by man, and man himself. In addition, the invention of paper, the use of papyrus, has left a wealth of early writings and information open to interpretation. The discovery of the Rosetta Stone made it all that much easier.

The Rosetta Stone

Manetho who was alive in very approximately 300 B.C., almost certainly had material of historical significance available to him that has since either been lost or destroyed. He started his history of Egypt from the time it was united into a single country by King Menes, approximately 3000 B.C., and listed 31 dynastic periods, each dynasty corresponding more or less to a period of one family.

Other "King Lists" are known as the Turin Canon of Kings (located in the Turin museum); the Palermo Stone (located in Palermo), though probably fragments of the Palermo Stone are (more appropriately) to be found in the Cairo museum; and the Table of Abydos which covers a wall in the Temple of King Sethos 1 at Abydos. In the latter list, the hieroglyphics describing a king's name appear in the typical oval frame that forms a *cartouche*, and the wall was used as a form of ancestor worship. The Table of Karnak at Thebes, the Table of Sakkara have both complemented Manetho's list.

King Lists, however, were not intended as historical records but as objects for temple rituals and may well have "delisted" the undeserving or the undesirable, including foreigners such as the Hyksos kings, and those who revered the "wrong" gods, such as Akhenaten who favored the god Aten.

These dynasties have since been grouped into periods:

Archaic Period: Dynasties 1 and 2

Old Kingdom: Dynasties 3 to 6. Considered as the development of a structured society

First Intermediate Period: Dynasties 7 to 11 when society collapsed

Middle Kingdom: Dynasty 12 when strong rulers restored structure to Egyptian society

Second Intermediate Period: Dynasties 13 to 17, government failed and foreigners came

New Kingdom: Dynasties 18 to 20, Egypt was restored to an even greater empire

Third Intermediate Period: Dynasties 21 to 25, the decline experienced by all empires

Last Period: Dynasties 26 to 31, Assyrian invasion followed by Greeks and Romans.

PREHISTORIC PERIODS

In archaeology and anthropology, human prehistory is subdivided around the three-age system.

1. The Stone Age
   Palaeolithic Age

Lower Palaeolithic

Middle Palaeolithic

Upper Palaeolithic

Mesolithic Age

Neolithic Age

The Copper Age was not part of the original three-age system.

2. The Bronze Age
3. The Iron Age

The dates for each age can vary by region:

North Africa

Palaeolithic

Epipaleolithic

Neolithic c. 7500 B.C.

Iron Age

Roman

Sub-Saharan Africa

Earlier Stone Age

Middle Stone Age

Later Stone Age

Neolithic c. 4000 B.C.

Bronze Age (3500 B.C. – 600 B.C.)

Iron Age (550 B.C. – AD 700)

Classic Middle Ages (c. 700 – 1700)

Near East Levantine

Stone Age (2,000,000 B.C. – 3300 B.C.)

Bronze Age (3300 B.C. – 1200 B.C.)

Iron Age (1200 B.C. – 586 B.C.)

Historical periods (586 B.C. – present)

DYNASTIES OF ANCIENT EGYPT

Early Dynastic Archaic Period

• 1st Dynasty (ca. 3000 – 2890 B.C.)

• 2nd Dynasty (2890–2686 B.C.)

Old Kingdom

• 3rd Dynasty (2686–2613 B.C.)

• 4th Dynasty (2613–2494 B.C.)

• 5th Dynasty (2494–2345 B.C.)

• 6th Dynasty (2345–2181 B.C.)

First Intermediate

• 7th Dynasty (2181–2160 B.C.)

• 8th Dynasty (2181–2160 B.C.)

• 9th Dynasty (2160–2025 B.C.)

• 10th Dynasty (2160–2025 B.C.)

• 11th Dynasty (Thebes only) (2125–2055 B.C.)

Middle Kingdom

• 11th Dynasty (All Egypt) (2055–1985 B.C.)

• 12th Dynasty (1985–1773 B.C.)

• 13th Dynasty (1773–1649 B.C.)

• 14th Dynasty (1773–1650 B.C.)

Second Intermediate

• 15th Dynasty (1650–1550 B.C.)

• 16th Dynasty (1650–1580 B.C.)

• 17th Dynasty (1580–1550 B.C.)

New Kingdom

• 18th (1550–1295 B.C.)

• 19th (1295–1186 B.C.)

• 20th (1186–1069 B.C.)

Third Intermediate

• 21st (1069–945 B.C.)

• 22nd (945–715 B.C.)

• 23rd (818–715 B.C.)

• 24th (727–715 B.C.)

• 25th (747–656 B.C.)

Late Period

• 26th (664–525 B.C.)

• 27th (1st Persian Period) (525–404 B.C.)

• 28th (404–399 B.C.)

• 29th (399–380 B.C.)

• 30th (380–343 B.C.)

• 31st (2nd Persian Period) (343–332 B.C.)

• **Argead** (332–305 B.C.)

• **Ptolemaic** (305–30 B.C.)

Prehistoric Era (700,000-4,000 B.C.)

Ancient Egypt was not geophysically the same as today's Egypt; the climate was not as dry, but the Nile was not as full, and there were probably permanent lakes in the Western Desert. It did, however, present a channel for *Homo Erectus* to travel northwards from the Rift Valley.

Many human-employed artifacts such as stone hand axes from the Lower Paleolithic era have been found in gravel deposits, but so far, no human remains to match them. However, the ease with which they are found in considerable quantities suggests there was a moderately large population using them.

From the Middle Paleolithic period are known animal bones, crocodiles, elephants, deer and rabbits with evidence that humans inhabited caves. A child's burial from the Middle Paleolithic period has been found, probably the oldest in Africa, and "stone mines" have been unearthed showing evidence of organized activity.

Upper Paleolithic stone quarries and underground galleries have been found, together with hearths and remnants of stone chipping activities; a buried body was found next to the mine, an axe head next to the deceased's own head.

Many Late Paleolithic sites in Upper (South) Egypt are known, but none in Lower (North) Egypt. They suggest repeated use by hunter-gatherers with discovered remnants of edible plants and grinding stones, evidence of fishing and animal hunting. Pits containing charcoal suggest fish may have been smoked for preservation in the later seasons. Large cemeteries are known with well-preserved skeletal remains, some of whom clearly met their death by trauma with stone axes. Questionable "rock art" has been found, dated to this period.

The earliest Neolithic sites are in the Western Desert where there were small lakes, with evidence of cattle herding, plant gathering but not agriculture; potsherds are also found. Numerous Middle and Late Neolithic sites show advances in stone tool design and in pottery making. Megaliths dating to this period have been found. In the later periods there is evidence of herding of other domesticated animals such as goats.

Development thereafter is largely related to techniques in pottery, found in numerous scattered areas in Upper and Lower Egypt and designated by the names of current habitations.

Archaic Period (3000-2686 B.C.)

DYNASTIES 1 & 2

Warfare between Upper (South) and Lower (North) Egypt had been the custom, but King Narmer of Upper Egypt overcame the inhabitants of the Delta region, the Kingdoms of Upper and Lower Egypt were joined. It is (currently) believed that King Narmer (3100–3050 B.C.) is identified with "Menes" who united Egypt and founded the first complete kingdom – the multiplicity of names does not make Egyptology easy to follow. He is identified with the royal hawk god, Horus, a title the king used, but which also gave rise to a set of parallel "Horus Names," such that most kings went by at least two names. As Horus, he was divine, a god on earth, reinforced by "Son of Re" the sun god.

King Narmer, from the Narmer Palette. Double Crown is seen. Photo by Keith Schengili-Roberts.

Narmer is represented wearing the double crown, composed of the lotus flower representing Upper Egypt and the papyrus reed representing Lower Egypt, on another representation wearing the red crown of Lower Egypt, signs of the unified rule of both parts of Egypt which was followed by all succeeding rulers.

In mythology, the unification of Egypt is portrayed as the hawk god Horus, identified with

Lower Egypt, as conquering and subduing the god Seth, who was identified with Upper Egypt.

Before the unification of Egypt, the land was settled with autonomous villages. With the early dynasties, and for much of Egypt's history thereafter, the country came to be known as the Two Lands.

Government

The rulers established a national administration and appointed royal governors. The capital of the two kingdoms moved from Abydos to Memphis, where a mud brick palace served both as royal residence and offices for the bureaucracy. Separate White House and Red House treasuries received taxation from the Two Lands.

Worship and Deities

The city of Thinis remained a center of worship.

The religious buildings were believed to be slightly more grand than normal village dwellings, only later did they become stone temples. Pit graves were used for burial of the working class. A much more elaborate structure was built for the rulers as "dwellings for the deceased," into which were inserted all the goods needed for the next world, together with sacrifice of personnel and animals to accompany the king; the practise of live sacrifice was discontinued after the first dynasty and replaced with images. The *mastaba* tombs of royalty were cut into rock, further fashioned with brick walls and divided into chambers. Royal servants and senior bureaucrats had similar tombs, but diminished in grandeur according to rank. The bodies decayed because they were not in contact with sand, but a decayed body did not meet the needs of the afterlife; it is in this period that early evidence of mummification to preserve bodies is first found. The bodies were wrapped, their image was painted on the wrappings, and even though the body within the shell deteriorated to a skeleton, the outward appearance in life was preserved. Needless to add, such attention was available only for royalty and the most important personages of society.

Gods provided a protective role for the ruler.

Horus was the supreme god who maintained a continuing rivalry with the god Seth, variously favored by different kings. Re was the great sun god whose cult center was at Iwnw (Heliopolis to the Greeks).

Image of Horus, from the Temple of Horus at Edfu. Photo by Ad Meskens.

There were two female goddesses, from each of the Two Lands, Edjo and Nekhbet. Neith was goddess of hunting and war; Seshat goddess of writing.

Ptah with a human form created the world, his worship center was at Memphis.

Gods with animal forms from different parts of the Two Lands were: Thoth (ibis headed moon god, patron of writing); Anubis (jackal god of cemeteries); Wepwawet (wolf god of war and death); Min (fertility god).

Technology

Egyptian written symbols indicated weights and materials such as grains, critical to early urban society; in the course of the first three dynasties it progressed to comprise more than 200 symbols.

There appeared pottery, bearing characteristics of the Southern Levant, and presumably indicating trade relationships. Copper came into use, as did refinement in brick making. A critical development in carpentry, in particular naval architecture, was the development of the mortise and tenon joint.

Old Kingdom (2686-2125 B.C.)

DYNASTIES 3 TO 6

It must be understood that the divisions of the dynasties into periods and terms such as "kingdoms" are entirely the creation of historians and Egyptologists, they were not known as such to the ancients of Egypt.

In the period designated "Old Kingdom," Egypt moved from tribal structure to a highly organized and centralized theocracy, the advantage of which was to confer on the ruler total power and thereby the ability to create massive works, such as the building of pyramids, but by no means were the works confined to these activities.

The king was placed mid-way between man and god, half of each, and had total control of everything and everyone in Egypt. Only the king could expect an individual eternity, and the efforts of the nation were directed to ensure his comfort, for the whole welfare of the population was dependent on the "survival" of the king.

But even the king was subject to the rules of precedent and the wishes of Ma'at, the goddess of order, truth and justice.

Clearly the tasks of ruling were beyond the control of a single person, and much was downloaded to the bureaucracy, most of whom were family. The senior bureaucrat was the vizier. Local governors were responsible for their districts (called *nomes*). The major element of the bureaucracy was housed in the capital city Ineb-Hedg (much later called Memphis), from which city were also controlled the systems of temples, granaries, public works, and pyramids.

Craftsmen also were centralised in Memphis, best known for the jewellery, pottery and other objects found in the burial chambers, which cannot have been all that they produced.

The bulk of the population worked the land. For the three months of the year when the land was flooded and unworkable, they may have worked instead at building pyramids; alternatively the pyramids were built by forced labor. Like so much about ancient Egypt, no one knows for sure and both possibilities may have been true at different times or in different places.

Trade

Egypt at the time of the Old Kingdom was intent on establishing trade relations with its neighbors, rather than warring with them.

The accepted southern boundary of Upper (southern) Egypt was the First Cataract at Elephantine. South of that lay Nubia, with which country Egypt traded her cereals, honey and manufactured goods for Nubia's building stone and gold.

Expeditions went to Punt which straddled the lower reaches of the Red Sea, to trade for spices, frankincense and myrrh. Ships sailed to Lebanon (Phoenicia) for their cedar wood. Ship builders of that era did not use wooden pegs or metal fasteners, but employed rope to support the framework, although the mortise and tenon joint was known.

External threat

There were military threats from across the Sinai peninsula where lived the "Sand Dwellers" and others classed as Asiatics from Palestine. There was no standing army. Peasants might be "drafted" as needed, and soldiers were also recruited from Nubia.

Religion

An unavoidable feature of moving from a primitive dispersed society to a more organized and centralized society, is the inheritance of a multiplicity of local deities, to each of which is attached a cult, on each of which a coterie of priests is dependent for their living, priests after all can't be expected to do manual labor.

The priests of Heliopolis, Memphis, and Hermopolis, and doubtless other lesser religious centers, all claimed priority for their own set of gods and creators of the universe. Re the sun god, became the pre-eminent deity. In earlier dynasties it was believed the king joined the gods as an equal, in later dynasties it was believed he travelled the seas of heaven in a boat with the gods but needed to return to earth periodically for sustenance, always kept available in the pyramids.

The Pyramid

Although the word "pyramid" is Greek, based on the shape of a wheat cake, the word the Egyptians used was *mer* meaning a Place of Ascension (not unlike the Christian belief).

The pyramid had its origins in Dynasty 3, when Imhotep, vizier to King Zoser expanded on the previous *mastaba* design by building six of them, one on top of another, each of decreasing size. This "stepped pyramid" at Sakkara (also spelled as Saqqara) is the oldest known stone building of substantial size. It is the center of a complex of buildings, some of which are twinned possibly to indicate the Two Lands.

The Stepped Pyramid at Saqqara. Photo by Charles J. Sharp.

Later, pyramids went from additional numbers of stepped *mastaba* to filling in the ledges with stones, smoothing off the surface and whitening it with limestone.

The most known pyramids were built at Giza by Cheops, son of Sneferu, not only because of their proximity to Memphis and the available flat land, but for the local availability of limestone. In later years the limestone was removed from all pyramids, for other building purposes, and exposed both the good and the not so good building qualities beneath.

The Great Pyramid of Giza.

As happened later with certain cathedrals, hubris combined with lack of engineering skills caused a massive collapse of a pyramid.

Each king had not only to build a pyramid for his own personal disposition, but he had also to maintain and do reverence for all of his predecessors' pyramids, so when it came to Shepseskaf he reverted to the modest Mastabat Fara'un traditional *mastaba* tomb; however, his successors in Dynasty 5 were not satisfied and continued with pyramid building at Abusir, which are judged as of inferior design. Coincident with the decrease in quality of pyramid was an increase in magnificence of temple design and decoration, hinting that power may have swung from king to priest.

By Dynasty 6, the king seemed to have doubted his immortality and the walls are covered with magic inscriptions aimed at consolidating his future in the afterlife.

The non-pyramid *mastaba* remained the funeral place for the non-kings, and gained increasingly in design, decoration and expense, as dynasty by dynasty, those associated with power became themselves more powerful. There was the belief that non-kings would continue with some form of existence within their burial chamber, hence the need for foodstuffs and support with items of a luxurious life.

The Old Kingdom destroyed itself. Initially the king owned everything, but as he made gifts of land and other property, exempt from taxation, to his courtiers, his own wealth, and the wealth of the country was diminished. Then there was the impossibility of the pyramid system – each pyramid required a staff and expenses to maintain it, no pyramid was ever "retired from service." Clearly that was an unmanageable system, which required only a period of time to elapse before it collapsed. Further decrees exempting persons and groups from taxation further diminished the national treasury. The switch of power from the king to the ennobled class is demonstrated by the decline in the structure of the pyramids while *pari passu* the nobles' *mastaba* increased in elegance. Nobles began to develop hereditary positions, and when the king married into the family of the nobility his god-like status was destroyed.

Culture

During the period designated Old Kingdom the skills of the builders, masons and stone carvers were developed and refined. The pyramids are massive, but the statues and paintings depicting people and animals continue to amaze the world in the excellence of their execution.

Much of the artistic labor was devoted to the "life after death" requirements of tombs, but there remain plenty of artefacts to show jewellery and furniture which enhanced the pleasure of mundane life.

End Game

In the 6th dynasty civil wars broke out due to disobedience of the nome governors, no longer members of the royal family. A severe drought 2200 to 2150 B.C. stayed the normal flooding of the Nile, resulting in many years of famine and breakdown in civil order, described on a tomb early in the First Intermediate Period.

The final collapse came when King Pepy (also spelled Pepi) II who ruled for 90 years could not contain invasion by "Asiatics."

First Intermediate Period (2160-2055 B.C.)

DYNASTIES 7 to 11

The central government is overthrown, provincial governors war against each other and anarchy overtakes Egypt, which explains why there is so little remaining in the way of artifacts to describe this dismal century in the history of ancient Egypt.

Some understanding of the progress of the chaos is gained by knowledge of European history when famine and disease decimated the population and the survivors turned to banditry, it is reflected in the description given in the papyrus (in the Leiden museum) called "Admonitions of a Prophet," and in another called, "Dispute with his Soul of One who is Tired of Life."

There was more than one factor that led to the anarchy: the irrigation from the Nile failed and in consequence the physical work of the irrigation system was neglected; King Pepy II was old and out of touch with reality; the governors of the provinces (*nomarchs* who governed *nomes*) had developed inherited powers and measures of independence; the kingdom could not prevent "Asiatics" from invading across the Sinai Peninsula and into the delta of Lower Egypt; foreign trade diminished and with it revenue decreased.

Resulting from the anarchy, the dead were left unburied and the tombs were desecrated. The discrediting of kingship was followed by the belief in an eternal life for the non-king, descending gradually to the commoner who thought he too was entitled to immortality, and here the god Osiris took prominence, his followers believing he could grant them their immortality.

Manetho in his King List described 70 kings who ruled for 70 days, in Dynasties 7 &8, presumably an indication of a chaotic state rather than fact.

Dynasties 9 & 10 each had 19 kings thought to have origin in Libya, invaders from the West who overwhelmed the weak Memphis rulers, established their rule at Heracleopolis, where they remained established for the next 600 years.

The founder of the ninth dynasty, King Akhtoy (aka Kheti 1) was described (he was a foreigner!) in terms of disapprobation by Manetho in his King List, and was said to have ended his days in madness, and killed by a crocodile.

It is noted that during this period the level of fine craftsmanship fell off, but was replaced by a form of provincial, naïve, art with freedom of expression released from state control. In contrast the literary forms of craft improved, and although chaos was found in much of the country during that century, tombs in Heracleopolis were decorated with texts describing not only the progress of the wars but more mundane activities such as the systems of irrigation and farming, and the diurnal activities of the royal family such as the children swimming.

Not all *nomes* were chaotic, the governor of Siut which lay between the territories of Thebes and Heracleopolis was recorded as digging canals, reducing taxation, reaping rich harvests, raising cattle herds, and maintaining an army and fleet, despite being the immediate target for Thebes invasions to the North.

Intef (aka Inyotef) *nomarch* of Thebes, brought together the other *nomarchs* of Upper Egypt and was the progenitor of his namesakes Kings Intef II & III who captured Abydos in Middle Egypt, and led the attacks into Lower Egypt.

Dynasty XI

Civil war with the rulers from Thebes continued until Mentuhotep Nebhepetre of Thebes defeated the forces of Heracleopolis and in Dynasty 11 Egypt was once again united as a single country, with Thebes as the capital city.

The dynasty traces its origins to a nomarch of Thebes, "Intef the Great, son of Iku." However, his immediate successor Mentuhotep I is considered the first king of this dynasty.

An inscription carved during the reign of Wahankh Intef II shows he was the first of this dynasty to claim to rule over the whole of Egypt. Intef undertook several campaigns northwards, and captured the important nome of Abydos.

Warfare continued intermittently between the Thebean and Heracleapolitan dynasts until the fourteenth regnal year of Mentuhotep II, when the Herakleopolitans were defeated, and this dynasty could begin to consolidate their rule. The rulers of Dynasty XI reasserted Egypt's influence over her neighbors in Africa and the Near East. Mentuhotep II sent renewed expeditions to Phoenicia to obtain cedar, Egypt was chronically short of wood..

The struggle was to be concluded by Mentuhotep II, during his fourteenth regnal year, he took advantage of a revolt in the Thinite Nome to launch an attack on Herakleopolis, which met little resistance. After toppling the last rulers of the 10th Dynasty, Mentuhotep began consolidating his power over all Egypt, a process which he finished by his 39th regnal year. Mentuhotep II commanded military campaigns south as far as the Second Cataract in Nubia, which had gained its independence during the First Intermediate Period. He also restored Egyptian hegemony over the Sinai region, which had been lost to Egypt since the end of the Old Kingdom. To consolidate his authority, he restored the cult of the ruler, depicting himself as a god in his own lifetime, wearing the headdresses of Amun and Min. He died after a reign of 51 years, and passed the throne to his son, Mentuhotep III.

Mentuhotep III reigned for only twelve years, during which he continued consolidating Theban rule over the whole of Egypt, building a series of forts in the eastern Delta region to secure Egypt against threats from Asia. He also sent an expedition to Punt by means of ships constructed at the end of Wadi Hammamat, on the Red Sea.

Contemporary records refer to "seven empty years" following the death of Mentuhotep III, which correspond to the reign of Mentuhotep IV.

Mentuhotep IV name is omitted from all ancient Egyptian king lists. The Turin Papyrus claims that after Mentuhotep III come "seven kingless years." Despite this absence, his reign is attested from a few inscriptions in Wadi Hammamat that record expeditions to the Red Sea coast and to quarry stone for the royal monuments. The leader of this expedition was his vizier Ammenemes, who is widely assumed to be the future pharaoh Ammenemes I, the first king of the 12th Dynasty.

Mentuhotep IV's absence from the king lists has prompted the theory that Ammenemes I usurped his throne. While there are no contemporary accounts of this struggle, certain circumstantial evidence may point to the existence of a civil war at the end of the 11th dynasty. What is certain is that, however he came to power, Ammenemes I was not of royal birth.

Middle Kingdom (1991-1786 B.C.)

12TH DYNASTY

There are varying definitions of the period of the Middle Kingdom, some authorities have it inclusive from the 11th to 14th Dynasties, here we follow those who use the term only for the 12th Dynasty.

After the collapse of the Old Kingdom, Egypt entered a period of weak Pharaonic power and decentralization called the First Intermediate Period. Towards the end of this period, two rival dynasties, known as the Tenth and Eleventh, fought for power over the entire country. The Theban 11th Dynasty only ruled southern Egypt from the first cataract to the Tenth Nome of Upper Egypt. To the north, Lower Egypt was ruled by the rival 10th Dynasty from Herakleopolis.

Ammenemes I (aka Amenemhat)

Ammenemes adopted the god Amun for his Dynasty, changing from Monyu, god of war, revered by his predecessors. Amun was identified with the fertility god, Min, worshiped at Thebes. The capital, however, was moved from Thebes to It Tqwy, south of the Delta region to give better control of Lower Egypt; a new royal cemetery was established on the west bank of the Nile where is now found the village of Lisht.

To strengthen the family's position on the throne King Ammenemes created his son, Sesostris I, as co-regent, he shared responsibilities with his father and thereby established himself as ruler; this precedent was later followed in other reigns.

His armies campaigned south as far as the Second Cataract of the Nile and into southern Canaan. He also re-established diplomatic relations with the Canaanite state of Byblos and Hellenic rulers in the Aegean Sea. Early in his reign he was compelled to campaign in the Delta region, which had not received as much attention as Upper Egypt during the 11th Dynasty. In addition, he strengthened defenses between Egypt and Asia, building the Walls of the Ruler in the East Delta region.

He campaigned also in the south against incursions by "C Group" a name currently given to the invaders from Nubia who blocked access of Egypt to the critical materials of gold and building stone. Fortresses were built on the Nile, at each of the cataracts, and were well staffed with soldiers.

From the 12th dynasty, Pharaohs maintained well-trained standing armies, which included Nubian contingents, and formed the basis of larger forces raised for defence against invasion, or for expeditions up the Nile or across the Sinai. The Middle Kingdom was basically defensive in its military strategy, with fortifications built at the First Cataract of the Nile, in the Delta and across the Sinai Isthmus.

Perhaps in response to this perpetual unrest, Ammenemes I built a new capital for Egypt in the north, known as Ammenemes Itj Tawy, or Ammenemes, Seizer of the Two Lands. The location of this capital is unknown, but is presumably near the city's necropolis, the present-day el-Lisht.

Ammenemes never held the absolute power commanded (in theory) by the Old Kingdom pharaohs. During the First Intermediate Period, the governors of the nomes of Egypt, (nomarchs) gained considerable power. Their posts had become hereditary, and some nomarchs entered into marriage alliances with the nomarchs of neighboring nomes. To strengthen his position, Ammenemes required registration of land, modified nome borders, and appointed nomarchs directly when offices became vacant, but acquiesced to the nomarch system, probably in order to placate the nomarchs who supported his rule. This gave the Middle Kingdom a more feudal organization than Egypt had before or would have afterwards.

Ammenemes was remembered for the mortuary temple at Hawara that he built, known to Herodotus, Diodorus, and Strabo as the "Labyrinth." During his reign the marshy Faiyum was first exploited.

Sesostris 1 (aka Senusret)

Sesostris I was campaigning against Libyan invaders when he received news of his father's death, and presumed murder. He immediately returned to Itj Tawy to ensure no other person would seize the government. During his reign he continued the practice of directly appointing nomarchs, and undercut the autonomy of local priesthoods by building cult centers throughout Egypt. Under his rule, Egyptian armies pushed south into Nubia as far as the second cataract, and incorporated northern Nubia as an Egyptian colony. To the west, he consolidated his power over the Oases, and to the north east he extended trading contacts with Palestine.

When he had held the throne for 46 years, Sesostris appointed Ammenemes II as coregent, and died three years later.

Ammenemes II

The events of this reign have gone largely unrecorded, there continued to be skirmishes and trading with neighboring countries, the nomarchs continued to be a problem and probably were in the ascendancy again. He appointed his son Sesostris II coregent.

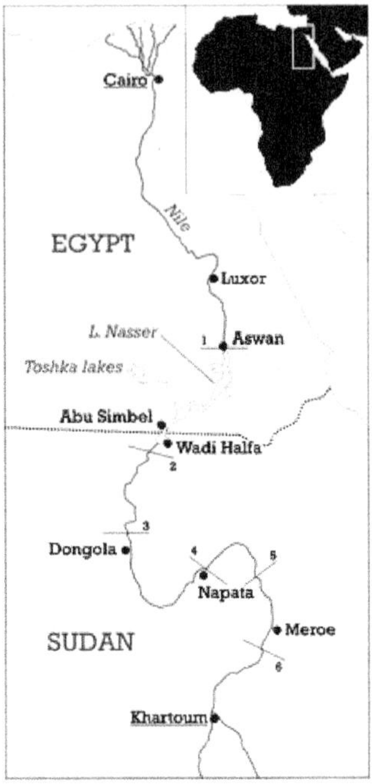

Cataracts of the Nile (1 – 6).

Sesostris II

Known as one of Egypt's greatest rulers, Sesostris II focused on domestic issues, particularly the irrigation of the Faiyum, a multi-generational project aimed to convert the Faiyum oasis into productive farmland.

Sesostris placed his pyramid at the site of el-Lahun, near the junction of the Nile and the Faiyum's major irrigation canal, the Bahr Yussef. Despite innovations in the pyramid to thwart grave robbers, they found their way to raid his tomb, but modern grave robbers (Egyptologists) found a wonderful store of jewellery where his princesses were entombed.

Like his predecessors, Sesostris also sent military expeditions into Nubia and trading expeditions into the Levant.

Sesostris III

Sesostris III continued the interminable war with Nubia, facilitating the movement of his troops by dredging an old canal around the first cataract. He added to the system of forts on the Nile, where the soldiers controlled movements of the local population, permitting them to trade with the forts' occupants, but preventing them from ascending the Nile by boat and preventing them from grazing their herds.

He reorganized the administration of Egypt by the creation of three bureaucracies to replace the nomarchs' power. Egypt was divided into three *waret*, North, South, and Head of the South, with a full and separate cabinet and council for each division.

His son Ammenemes III participated in a long co-regency with his father.

Ammenemes III

Ammenemes III benefited from the military and trading acumen of the previous rulers of the Twelfth Dynasty, and his reign was marked by Egypt`s prosperity. His reign is remarkable for the degree to which Egypt exploited its resources. Permanent dwellings for miners have been unearthed together with extensive cemeteries. He continued the drainage of swampland at Faiyum, and many monuments were built, but the introduction of 'Asiatic' laborers set the scene for later troubles. He also supported and strengthened the defense works against Nubia.

Ammenemes IV

During the reign of Ammenemes IV the records of the level of water and flooding periods of the Nile showed they were insufficient for irrigation. This might have indicated hunger and the drawing to a close of prosperity.

Queen Sobekneferu

Queen Sobekneferu was the first known female sovereign of Egypt. She had no heirs, when she died the Twelfth Dynasty came to an end.

Achievements of the Middle Kingdom

Administration

After Egypt was reunited at the end of the Eleventh Dynasty, the king appointed chief ministers, Viziers, one for Upper and one for Lower Egypt. Other positions, equivalent to cabinet rank were the Overseer of Sealed Goods (Treasurer), Overseer of the Estate (King's chief steward), and Scribe of the Royal Document (King's writer).

Agriculture and climate

The years of repeated high flood levels of the Nile correspond to the most prosperous period of the Middle Kingdom, which occurred during the reign of Ammenemes III, conversely recorded low levels corresponded with famine and unrest. For this reason the reclamation of arable land at Faiyum was important to the nation's prosperity.

Life Style

At a village the discoverer called Kahun, though known to its inhabitants as "Sesostris is content," there was unearthed all the paraphernalia of daily life for those who built the pyramids, including craftsmen's tools, looms, equipment for spinning, children's toys.

Literature

Egyptian literature was not recorded in written form until the early Twelfth Dnasty of the Middle Kingdom when the classical form of hieroglyphs was devised and became the "copybook" models for children's education. Old Kingdom texts served mainly to maintain the divine cults, preserve souls in the afterlife, and document accounts for practical uses in daily life. It was not until the Middle Kingdom that texts were written for the purpose of entertainment and intellectual curiosity.

It is also thought that the growth of the middle class and a growth in the number of scribes needed for the expanded bureaucracy under Sesostris II helped spur the development of Middle Kingdom literature, ancient Egyptians considered the literature from this time as "classic."

"Instructions in Wisdom" was effectively political propaganda lauding the power of the king. The concept of the short story was born. Stories such as the Tale of the Shipwrecked Sailor and the Story of Sinuhe were composed during this period, and were popular enough to be widely copied afterwards. Many philosophical works were also created at this time.

Funerals

Mummification during the time of the Old Kingdom did not require removal of viscerae, and the bodies deteriorated. By the time of the Middle Kingdom the rites had advanced, bodies were coated with preservative but were not eviscerated, and they have not survived. Bodies were placed in a double coffin, one shaped like the body, the other a rectangular box; both were highly decorated.

Second Intermediate Period (1650-1550 B.C.)

DYNASTIES 13 to 17

As previously remarked, there is a difference of opinion between scholars on what constitutes the Second Intermediate Period, some include only Dynasties 14 to 17, here we will include Dynasty 13 in this period.

Like the First Intermediate Period, the Second is marked by national disorganization and a number of overlapping reigns in fragmented portions of Egypt. It also was a period when for a time a portion of Egypt was controlled by foreign rulers, that is to say non-ethnic Egyptians, called the Hyksos.

Manetho describes 60 kings of Dynasty 13 whose rule was based on Thebes, the term dynasty is misleading, as most kings of the thirteenth dynasty were not related. Contemporaneous was Dynasty 14, 76 kings whose rule was based in the Delta, and the foreign Hyksos rulers who comprised Dynasties 15 and 16. In Dynasty 17 the foreigners were driven out and control of the whole of Egypt was returned for Dynasty 18 which founded the New Kingdom..

After allowing discipline at the southern forts to deteriorate, the government eventually withdrew its garrisons and, not long afterward, the forts were re-occupied by the rising Nubian state of Kush. In the north, Lower Egypt was overrun by the Hyksos, a Semitic people from across the Sinai.

Hyksos

The origin and meaning of the word is argued between "foreign rulers," and "shepherd kings," but they were "Asiatic" in the sense of east of Sinai, although they had been filtering into Egypt for some long time either as laborers, skilled artisans or prisoners of war kept for slave labor. The Hyksos first appeared in Egypt during the eleventh dynasty, in the thirteenth dynasty they gained power, and in the second intermediate period they controlled the Delta. Not until the end of the seventeenth dynasty were they expelled. There are many romantic tales about their origin, with biblical connotations, but they were probably of several different ethnicities, dominantly Semitic.

The Hyksos kingdom was centered in the eastern Nile Delta and Middle Egypt and was limited in size, never extending south into Upper Egypt, which was under the control of Theban-based rulers. Hyksos relations with the south seem to have been mainly of a commercial nature, although Theban princes appear to have recognized the Hyksos rulers and may possibly have provided them with tribute for a period. The Hyksos Fifteenth Dynasty rulers established their capital and seat of government at Avaris.

The rule of these kings overlaps with that of the native Egyptian pharaohs of the 16th and 17th dynasties of Egypt. The first pharaoh of the 18th dynasty, Ahmose I, finally expelled the Hyksos from Gaza by the 16th year of his reign. In spite of the prosperity that the stable political situation brought to the land, the native Egyptians continued to view the Hyksos as non-Egyptian, so when they were eventually driven out of Egypt, all traces of their occupation were erased. No accounts survive recording the history of the period from the Hyksos perspective, only that of the native Egyptians who evicted the occupiers, in this case the rulers of the Eighteenth Dynasty who were the direct successor of the Theban Seventeenth Dynasty.

Revolutionary methods of warfare ensured the Hyksos the ascendancy in their influx into the new empire being established in Egypt's delta and at Thebes in support of the Red Sea trade, such as the composite bow, the improved recurved bow, the horse-drawn war chariot, improved arrowheads, various kinds of swords and daggers, a new type of shield, mailed shirts, and the metal helmet.

The Seventeenth Dynasty

Around the time Memphis and Itj Tawy fell to the Hyksos, the native Egyptian ruling house in Thebes declared its independence from the vassal dynasty in Itj Tawy and set itself up as the seventeenth dynasty. This dynasty was to prove the salvation of Ancient Egypt and eventually would lead the war of liberation that drove the Hyksos back into Asia. The Theban based Seventeenth Dynasty restored numerous temples throughout Upper Egypt while maintaining peaceful trading relations with the Hyksos kingdom in the north. Senakhtenre Ahmose, the first king in the line of Ahmoside kings even imported white limestone from the Hyksos controlled region of Tura in Lower Egypt. However, his successor, Kamose, is credited with initiating the final defeat of the Hyksos since they launched the wars of liberation against the foreign Asiatic Hyksos kings. With the accession of Ahmose I, the New Kingdom period of Egypt begins. Ahmose I would succeed in expelling the Hyksos from Egypt and placing the country under a centralised administrative control for the first time since the mid-13th dynasty.

New Kingdom (1550-1069 B.C.)

DYNASTIES 18 to 20

The New Kingdom of Egypt is the period in ancient Egyptian history between the 16th and 11th centuries B.C., covering the Eighteenth, Nineteenth, and Twentieth Dynasties of Egypt. The New Kingdom followed the Second Intermediate Period and was succeeded by the Third Intermediate Period. It was Egypt's most prosperous time and marked the peak of its power.

The later part of this period, under the Nineteenth and Twentieth Dynasties (1292-1069 B.C.) is also known as the Ramesside period, after the eleven pharaohs who took the name of Ramesses.

Possibly as a result of the foreign rule of the Hyksos during the Second Intermediate Period, the New Kingdom saw Egypt attempt to create a buffer between the Levant and Egypt, and attained its greatest territorial extent. Similarly, in response to very successful 17th century attacks by the powerful Kingdom of Kush , the New Kingdom felt compelled to expand far south into Nubia and hold wide territories in the Near East. Egyptian armies fought Hittite armies for control of modern-day Syria.

Dynasty 18

The dynasty is sometimes known as the Thutmosid Dynasty because of the four pharaohs named Thutmosis (English: Thoth child). The pharaohs of Dynasty 18 ruled for approximately two hundred and fifty years, many were buried in the Valley of the Kings in Thebes.

Great importance was attached to close dynastic marriages and royal wives were of significance in this. Dynasty 18 was founded by Ahmosis I, whose parents were Sequenre Ta'o and Ahhotpe, in fact brother and sister. Ahmosis I married Ahmose-Nefertari, probably his niece, who like his mother became a powerful queen. The reign of Ahmosis I spans the Second Intermediate Period when the Hyksos were driven out of Egypt, and the New Kingdom.

Ahmosis was followed by his son, Amenophis I in whose reign were developed the various policies that formed the pattern of government in Dynasty 18. The capital city was based at Thebes, in part because victory over the Hyksos was attributed to the important god of Thebes, Amun, who became not only god of the air, but also fertility and warfare, and was associated with Re, the sun god in one form, Amen-Re, the creator and ruler of all people; Thebes was considered as the original site of creation, where Amun had begotten himself in secret. His temple at Karnak, Thebes, was of the utmost importance, and its priests gained power and wealth, with the inevitable negative eventual result of abuse of power to rival the Pharaoh.

In this dynasty the kings abandoned pyramid building and instead cut tombs deep into the rock of a narrow valley which Egyptologists have named, Valley of the Kings. With the exception of the tomb of Tutankhamun, all were pillaged. In Dynasty 18, queens were entombed in random areas, but later a Valley of the Queens was established, with similarly ornate tombs.

Amenophis I was followed by Tuthmosis I, who conquered north to the kingdom of the Mittani at Carchemish on the Euphrates, and beyond the fourth cataract of the Nile to the south. Thutmosis I was succeeded by Tuthmosis II and his queen, Hatshepsut. She was the daughter of Tuthmosis I and soon after her husband's death, ruled for over twenty years after becoming pharaoh during the minority of her stepson, and was referred to in the masculine gender. She herself mothered daughters but no son. During her reign (modern day) Palestine and Syria drove out the Egyptian invader. The stepson later became pharaoh as Tuthmosis III, and obliterated Hatshepsut's name from many of her monuments.

Tuthmosis III had a lengthy reign, he later became known as the greatest military pharaoh ever. He conducted 14 military campaigns in 16 years, and seems to have had his country permanently at war with her neighbors, reconquering and adding to the lands taken by Amenophis I. He had a second co-regency in his old age with his son Amenophis II, who also was famed in stela memorials for his military valor and accomplishments, including victories in Syria. Records show presentation of gifts by rulers of the Hittites, Assyria and Babylonia.

Tuthmosis III was succeeded by Tuthmosis IV, in whose reign the sundisk Aten became prominent as a deity; in his turn he was followed by his son Amenophis III.

The reign of Amenophis III is seen as a high point in this dynasty. Tribute was willingly given, conquest was at an end, and Egypt was considered the greatest power of the region. Amenophis III undertook large scale building programs, with a palace at Malkata on the west bank of the Nile at Thebes. Possibly to break from the power of the priests his principal wife was non-royal, came from outside the family, but he had numerous other wives, some of them princesses sent as "offerings" from tributary states.

Amenophis III may have shared the throne for up to 12 years with his son Amenophis IV, who would change his name to Akhenaten (servant of the Aten); Amenophis only came to this position due to the premature death of his older brother Tuthmosis. His queen was Nefertiti who possibly was a Mitannian princess sent to marry Amenophis III, but was certainly not of royal Egyptian stock. There are suggestions she had unprecedented power associated with the cult of worship of Aten, and it is known she adopted a new name, Neferneferuaten (Fair is the goddess of the Aten).

Image of Akhenaten.

Amarna period

During the reign of Akhenaten, the Aten (the sundisk and a facet of the god Re) first became the most prominent deity, and eventually the Aten was considered the only god, the first time monotheism was suggested. Priesthoods of other cults were disbanded (a step comparable to Henry VIII and the Dissolution of the Monasteries). In the fifth year of his reign Amenophis IV changed his name to Akhenaten and moved his capital to Amarna (aka Akhetaten – Horizon of the Aten) and now called Tell el-Amarna. A stretch of open unused land, eight miles wide, midway between Thebes and the Delta, east bank of the Nile, and uncontaminated by any previous residence of a god.

Later Egyptians considered the so-called Amarna Period an unfortunate aberration. Neither Nefertiti nor minor queens were able to produce sons, though numbers of daughters were born, even the daughters failed to produce male heirs, and the throne passed to two young princes of uncertain heritage, Smenkhare who had married Akhetaten's eldest daughter, ruled for a few months and at his death was succeeded by Tutankhaten, nine years old and married to Akhenaten's third daughter (widow of her father!). They died of unknown causes at the ages of 20 and 19 respectively. During Tutankhaten's young reign the priests set about undoing the damage Akhetaten had caused with the monotheistic worship of Aten, and the court moved back to Thebes. Tutankhaten changed his name to Tutankhamun which signified abandoning Aten. His fame is derived from the intact tomb discoveries in the Valley of the Kings, and not due to any action he undertook.

Tutankhamun's burial mask. Photo by Bjørn Christian Tørrissen.

Ay and Horemheb

Succession to the throne now became an issue. The royal widow, Ankhesenamun, appealed to the king of the Hittites despite the problem they were known as Egypt's enemy, asking him to send a son for her to marry and he would be Pharaoh. A Hittite prince was dispatched, and was murdered en route to Egypt. Ankhesenamun married a commoner, though a courtier, named Ay, who spent four years restoring the status quo ante Aten before he died.

His successor was Horemheb, a general during the reign of Tutankhamun, who reigned for 27 years during which time he terminated the Aten cult and destroyed the city of Akhenaten, even had its name expunged from the records. He placed loyal followers in power, had all the old gods restored, built a strong army, and passed a stable and prosperous kingdom to posterity. He had no children so he designated an army companion, Pa-Ramesses, to follow him.

Dynasty 19

Ramesses I

The Pharaohs of the 19th dynasty ruled for approximately one hundred and ten years. The first, Pa-Ramesses, who took the reign name, Ramesses I, had a son, Sethos (aka Seti), and perhaps it was the son that Horemheb had in mind for the future of Egypt. The dynasty is best known for its military conquests in Canaan.

The warrior kings of the early 18th Dynasty had encountered only little resistance from neighbouring kingdoms, allowing them to expand their realm of influence easily. The situation had changed radically towards the end of the 18th Dynasty. The Hittites gradually extended their influence into Syria and Canaan to become a major power in international politics, a power that both Sethos I and his son Ramesses II would need to deal with.

Sethos I

Sethos I launched an extensive building program, noticeable particularly for the temple to Osiris, and for the scenes of his military campaigns on the Hypostyle Hall at Karnak. He pursued war on all fronts, against the Hittites to the north, the Libyans to the west, and the Nubians to the south. He was buried in the Valley of the Kings, but grave robbers later brought his alabaster sarcophagus to London.

Ramesses II

Ramesses II, (called *The Great*) son of Sethos was thoughtfully given a harem by his father whom he served as co-regent, enabling him to father many children, but he outlived the oldest twelve of his sons. His wives included two Hittite princesses rendered as part of peace negotiations, and Queen Nefertari who was honoured by a beautiful tomb in the Valley of the Queens and a temple at Abu Simbel where buildings were erected to impress the Nubians with the might of Egypt. Ramesses II was possibly the Pharaoh at the time of the Israelites captivity in Egypt. Much of his military activity was conducted against the Hittites; eventually both sides came to a realization of the folly of war and the first peace treaty known to history was signed.

Statue of Ramesses II. Photo by Aymeric Lopez.

Merneptah

Merneptah was in his sixties when he ruled alone, but he had been co-ruler with his father for 12 years and was well versed in government. He became engaged in conflict with Libyans to the west who had formed an alliance with the Sea Peoples (whose exact origins are undefined) and were attempting to settle with their cattle and families in the Delta. Merneptah slaughtered many, but did not abolish the problem – when desperate people need land it is hard to deter them. There were also the perennial problems with Nubia.

After 10 years on the throne without a co-regent, Merneptah died and succession was confused. Amenmesse usurped the throne from Merneptah's son and designated successor, Sethos II, but he ruled Egypt for only four years. After his death, Sethos regained power and destroyed most of Amenmesse's monuments. He was followed on the throne by Siptah, probably a boy, and under the influence of a Syrian chancellor called Bay. When he died, Sethos' widow, Queen Twosret took the throne, but she proved unable to maintain her hold on power amid the conspiracies and power plays being hatched at the royal court. She was likely ousted in a revolt led by Setnakhte, founder of the Twentieth Dynasty.

Dynasty 20

Pharaoh Setnakhte was likely already middle aged when he took the throne after Queen Twosret (and he also took her tomb!). His brief reign was followed by his son Ramesses III who in his fifth year as Pharaoh had again to contend with the Sea Peoples (seafarers from the eastern Mediterranean) who he defeated and enslaved. Three years later they were back again, in confederation with the Libyans and with a significant fleet; once again, the Egyptians defeated them. There are papyrus records of his reign describing a strike by royal workmen, and others describing the trial of would-be assassins whose plot was instigated by a secondary wife, named Tiy who hoped to put her son Pentawere on the throne. The case was noteworthy in that five of the judges were complicit in the plot. Other documents from this period record investigation and punishment of the systematic robbing of the Royal Tombs.

The king may have died from the attempt on his life, but it was his legitimate heir Ramesses IV who succeeded him to the throne. After this a succession of kings named Ramesses take the throne, but none would truly achieve greatness. As happened under the earlier Nineteenth Dynasty, this group struggled under the effects of the bickering between the heirs of Ramesses III, three different sons are known to have assumed power as Ramesses IV, Ramesses VI and Ramesses VIII respectively. However, at this time Egypt was also increasingly beset by a series of droughts, below-normal flooding levels of the Nile, famine, civil unrest and official corruption.

The power of the last king, Ramesses XI, grew so weak that in the south the High Priests of Amun at Thebes became the *de facto* rulers of Upper Egypt, while Smendes controlled Lower Egypt even before Ramesses XI's death. Smendes would eventually found the Twenty-First dynasty at Tanis.

Third Intermediate Period (1069-664 B.C.)

DYNASTIES 21 to 25

During this period Egypt continued in a downward spiral, and for some of the time came under foreign rulers.

Dynasty 21

The death of Ramesses XI terminated Dynasty 20, he was followed by Nesbenebded who had effectively controlled the North, chose the name Smendes and founded Dynasty 21 with Tanis as his main residence, where was found superb treasures of gold and silver, vessels and jewellery, but poor preservation of human remains due to the climate.

Seven kings are listed by Manetho for the 21st Dynasty, but they ruled only in the North. The South was dominated by the high-priests of Amun, descended from a priest named Herihor; one of these priests, Pinudjem I, recognized Smendes as the Pharaoh and he in return accepted the priest Pinidjem as the ruler in the South. This was an amicable arrangement, the two families remained on good terms and intermarried, and arrangements were made for re-interment of desecrated mummies dating back to the New Kingdom to improve their chances of attaining immortality.

Dynasty 22

When Psusennes II, last ruler of Dynasty 21 died, in the absence of a direct male heir the throne passed to his son-in-law Shoshenk, an army commander, who became Shoshenk I of Dynasty 22, also termed the Bubastite dynasty after his home town, Bubastis. This family was of Libyan origin, but long settled in the Delta, and known as Meshwesh.

There is not a great deal known about this dynasty, perhaps due to the northern location of their capital where monuments were less well preserved than in the dry climate of the south. Thebes continued as the religious center in the south, and Shoshenk I had his second son, Iuput, made high-priest at Thebes, bringing that region of Egypt also under his control.

From Dynasty 22 were discovered sacred Apis-bulls in vast subterranean chambers; most kings of Dynasty 22 were buried at Tanis with magnificent treasures in their tombs.

Shoshenk I conducted trade excursions into Nubia and Byblos and military excursions into Palestine (described in the Bible as King Shishak taking treasure from Jerusalem).

Dynasty 23

According to Manetho, there were four kings in this dynasty. Their rule was centered on Tanis, possibly they were contemporaneous with Dynasty 22, and probably they had only regional power.

Dynasty 24

Manetho gives the name of only one king, Bochchoris of Sais in the Delta. He recorded that "a lamb spoke" in human voice to forecast the overthrow of Egypt by Assyria.

The rulers of this dynasty were descended from Tefnakhte, prince of Sais, of obscure origins; their attempt to expand their rule to the south was blocked by Piankhy who ruled a kingdom to the south of Egypt with a capital at Napata near the 4th cataract close to the mountain called Gebel Barkal.

It is determined from available records that Egypt was during this period fragmented and under several simultaneous rulers. Piankhy's brother, Shabako, came north to defeat the army of Bochchoris and founded Dynasty 25.

Dynasty 25

Sometimes known as the Ethiopian or Kushite Dynasty, it was founded by Shabako who invaded Egypt from the south, and set up the first dynasty of Nubian Pharaohs at Thebes as the capital and with Amen-Re as the principal god.

Taharka, considered the most effective ruler of this dynasty was crowned at Memphis. Egypt during his reign was both peaceful and prosperous attested by his extensive building programs in both Nubia and Egypt. However, he came into conflict with the Assyrians who now represented the major power in competition with Egypt, having submerged the Hittites.

Hezekiah, King of Judah, appealed to the Egyptians for help against the Assyrians, but Senacherib and his Assyrians defeated the Egyptian army at el-Tekeh.

In 674 B.C. the new ruler of Assyria, Esarhaddon who followed Senacherib after he was murdered, attempted an invasion of Egypt, but was repulsed by Taharka; he returned, however, in 671 B.C. and drove Taharka out of Memphis and back down to the south whence his dynasty had come. Esarhaddon destroyed Memphis, took booty and slaves, and appointed locals as his governors; one of these was Necho, prince of Sais.

Esarhaddon made further expedition against Egypt but died on campaign. The Egyptian king Taharka returned north and re-established his rule at Memphis. But the new Assyrian king, Ashurbanipal, in 622 B.C. regained Memphis and Taharka fled back to the south where he died.

Various princelings attempted to establish themselves, but Ashburnipal returned and took more booty after destroying buildings, and rebel princes were taken back to Nineveh. Taharka's nephew, Tanuatamum, attempted to establish an Egyptian kingdom in Memphis, but this resulted only in further retribution by Ashburnipal who not only drove Tanuatamum back to Nubia but stripped Thebes of all that could be removed. The Nubian kingdom shrank back to Nubia, with its northern boundary at the 3rd cataract

Divine Wife of Amun

The King's chief wife held this title, as such she participated in festivals but as consort to the god. From Dynasty 21 the title was instead given to the king's daughter, who acquired wealth and power with it, but because she was not allowed to marry she adopted the daughter of the next king as her successor, thus ensuring the succession of the king and precluding male rivals from seizing power.

Late Period (672-322 B.C.)

DYNASTY 26 to 31

The Assyrian king, Esarhaddon, had permitted a degree of local autonomy with native regional rulers, among the most powerful of whom was Necho I, prince of Sais, who established a small kingdom in the western Delta based on Sais. He was removed to Nineveh for disloyalty, then returned to power in the Delta by Ashburnipal, ruling as Necho 1. He was killed by the Nubian ruler Tanuatamun who regained Egypt and took Memphis.

Dynasty 26 (Sais)

Psammetichus, son of Necho I regained control and founded Dynasty 26. Various histories from other countries, including the Old Testament, recount incidents of these times. Psammetichus used Greek mercenaries to establish his power. Foreigners settled in Egypt, they caused dissatisfaction with locals, and districts such as Naucratis were established for them where they could carry on their separate lives and traditions.

During this period crafts flourished and the highest quality artifacts were produced. A waterway was established between the Nile and the Red Sea to facilitate trade; a fleet of triremes with Phoenician sailors, made a three year voyage around Africa, through the Red Sea around the Cape and back into the Mediterranean via Gibraltar.

The Assyrians who had conquered Egypt were now threatened by the Medes and Babylonians. Psammetichus who had ceased to pay tribute to the Assyrians now joined with them as their ally, which did not prevent the sacking of Nineveh.

Psammetichus' son, Necho II, fought against Josiah, the King of Judah, and took control of Jerusalem. But the Babylonians were now the power to contend with and after skirmishes in the region of the River Euphrates, the Egyptians were soundly defeated by the Babylonians under Nebuchadnezzar in 605 B.C. at Carchemish, and Egypt abandoned its conquered territories, only to defeat Nebuchadrezzar in further battles.

Necho II was followed by his son Psammetichus II who avoided external battles, and pursued programs of building. He was followed by his son Apries (called in the Bible Pharaoh Hophra). Apries sent an army into Libya at the request of the native population to remove the Greeks, however, this army was defeated by the Greek colonists in Cyrene, and he was deposed and replaced by a drunken but popular general, called Amasis. Apries was later killed.

Amasis was followed by his son Psammetichus III who reigned only for few months before he was defeated by Persians under Cambyses at Pelusium in 525 B.C.. Psammetichus III was killed and the Persians annexed Egypt converting it to a satrapy (province), under the authority of a Persian satrap (governor).

Dynasty 27 (Persian)

The Persian rule was not oppressive, there was an exchange of talents in both directions, and was a mutual cultural benefit.

Cambyses sent an army to the Siwa oasis which was lost to history.

Darius followed and was an understanding and beneficial ruler who supported Egypt's laws and gods, and completed the abandoned canal to the Red Sea.

Xerxes followed his father Darius in 486 B.C., and showed no interest in Egypt. After Xerxes murder, he was followed by Artaxerxes 465 B.C., some local disturbances in the Delta resulted in the Egyptian Inaros asking Athens for help against the Persians, but the armistice between Athenians and Persians put an end to that, though other local Egyptian chieftains persisted with resistance to the Persian rule.

Dynasty 28

Manethos lists Amyrtaeus as the only king of Dynasty 28.

Dynasty 29

Four kings from the town of Mendes are listed.

Dynasty 30

Three kings from the town of Sebennytus are listed.

Artaxerxes in 375 B.C. attempted a reconquest of Egypt but his general, Pharnabzus, was repulsed by flooding of the Nile, but on his next attempt in 343 B.C. the Persians destroyed the defensive walls of the cities, looted the temples of anything of value or interest, before returning to their home in Babylon.

Dynasty 31

This was the second period of Persian rule, and included the reigns of Artaxerxes III, his son Arses, and Darius III.

When Alexander the Great arrived in Egypt 332 B.C., Persia's rule was at an end.

Alexander Conquers Persia

Alexander's ascent to the throne of Macedon was not unopposed after his father's death. Fearful of political rivals challenging the claim of a young and relatively untested monarch whose father had died so suddenly and mysteriously, Alexander had many of his political rivals, chief among them those who had a tenable claim to the throne, executed. Olympias, who had returned from exile, also took advantage of the turmoil to have Cleopatra, Philip's widow, and her daughter by him, burned alive. It is also likely that she tried to poison Philip's son by Cleopatra, but a botched attempt (or perhaps natural causes) made him mentally disabled, and thus no longer a threat. For his part, Alexander was furious at this barbarity, which prompted an estrangement which lasted for years.

Alexander also had to contend with problems outside of Macedonia. News of the *Hegemon*'s death had not gone unnoticed, and virtually all of Philip's conquests rose up in arms: the Thracians, Thessalians, Athenians and Thebans all discarded their alliances with Macedon, rushing to occupy the passes in the north of Greece against Alexander's forces. Ignoring suggestions of a political solution to the uprising, Alexander led his cavalry on an encircling march around the Thessalian forces sent to bar his way, surrounding them and forcing them into surrender before marching southwards. The Greek city-states, terrified by the speed of his advantage, promptly sued for peace, recognising him as *Hegemon*. Alexander was formally invested with the title in the city of Corinth, where he also famously encountered the renowned philosopher Diogenes the Cynic. Alexander, who through his tutelage by Aristotle had developed an admiration for wise men, asked Diogenes if the King of Macedon might do anything for him. Diogenes, who was sitting in the public square at the time, sourly looked up at him and told Alexander that he could; he could get out of his sun. This remark prompted Alexander to later say, "If I could not be Alexander, I would be Diogenes". Plutarch would later write that Alexander and Diogenes died on the same day in 323 B.C.

His position in Greece now secure, Alexander turned northwards, and in 335 B.C. he succeeded in securing his northern frontiers for good in a lightning campaign which crushed the armies of the Thracians and Illyrians utterly in a series of vicious battles. It was a remarkable display of soldiering, but one that the Greek cities seemed content to ignore: while Alexander was occupied in the Balkans, Thebes and Athens rose in revolt once more, despite their promises of friendship. Furious, Alexander marched his army southwards. This time, despite the entreaties of many of his advisors, he would show no mercy. When Thebes, abandoned by Athens, continued to resist him, he razed the city to the ground. This effectively ended all further resistance in Greece, and with his position as *Hegemon* firmly established, Alexander decided it was time to pursue his father's dream; it was time to invade Persia.

Ever since the famous Persian invasions that had been repelled by the Athenians at Marathon and then by the Spartans at Thermopylae and Plataea, Greece and Persia had been at odds. For the past few years they had enjoyed an uneasy peace, but that peace was shattered when, in 334 B.C., Alexander crossed the Hellespont into Persia. He brought with him an army of 50,000 infantry, 6,000 cavalry and a navy of over 100 ships, a mixed force of Macedonians, Greeks, Thracians and Illyrians, all chosen for their specific strengths (the Thessalians, for example, were famous cavalrymen). This mongrel force would become Alexander's *modus operandi* for the remainder of his campaigns.

Alexander's invasion was immediately challenged. At the Granicus, in modern Turkey, Alexander crushed a force of 30,000 Persian troops sent to oppose him, and during the battle he led the cavalry himself, as he was accustomed to doing. The destruction of this Persian field army granted him control of virtually all the neighbouring territory, and he captured the city of Sardis before marching on the fortress of Halicarnassus, which fell after a vicious siege. From there, he proceeded into Lycia and Pamphylia, systematically conquering all the coastal territory of Asia Minor. He then marched inland, where he famously visited the city of Gordium, seat of a renowned temple. The temple housed a cart whose parts were held together by a supposedly unsolvable knot, and legend had it that any man who could untie it would be made King of Asia. Alexander, disdaining any attempt at trying to fumble at the knot with his fingers, simply drew his sword and hacked it in two.

After wintering in Asia Minor, Alexander crossed into the Persian heartland in 333 B.C. Finally moved to action by what he at least perceived as a serious threat, the Persian emperor Darius III mustered an army that most sources suggest numbered almost 100,000 men, and marched against Alexander. Battle was joined at Issus, in November of 333 B.C. The battle was vicious, and Alexander lost more than 7,000 men, but he annihilated the Persian army, inflicting more than 20,000 casualties upon them and forcing them to flee the field. Darius escaped in the rout, but Alexander's men captured his royal treasury, his wife, daughters and mother. Alexander disdainfully refused an offer from Darius of a peace treaty and land concessions, claiming that as he was now King of Asia, it fell to him to decide how to dispose of his possessions. Alexander then marched into Syria, which he conquered with relative ease, but his attempts at pacifying the region in short order were frustrated first by the city of Tyre and then again by the stronghold of Gaza. Both cities had colossal fortifications that required the construction of siege works and engines of war on a scale hitherto unseen to reduce, and the resistance from both garrisons was exceedingly fierce, prompting Alexander to kill all men of fighting age and sell survivors into slavery when they were finally taken. At Gaza, as Alexander personally led an attack against the walls, he was struck by a missile from above and seriously injured in the shoulder, one of the many serious wounds he was to accrue in his time as a fighting King.

Having witnessed the fate of Tyre and Gaza, the garrison of Jerusalem capitulated to Alexander without a fight, allowing him to push southwards into Egypt. The ancient kingdom of the Pharaohs had been reduced to a vassal state of Persia, and its inhabitants greeted Alexander like a liberator, the entire country falling to him without a fight. In 332 BC Alexander made a pilgrimage to the shrine of Siwa, in the Egyptian desert, where the Oracle proclaimed him ruler of the world and son of Ammon, the Egyptian patriarchal deity, leading Alexander to adopt the title "Son of Zeus Ammon". Coins minted by him, from there on out, showed him with ram's horns as a mark of his divine parentage. It is unclear whether Alexander truly believed the rumors of his own divinity, but it is undeniable that the Oracle's verdict severely inflated his pride, prompting the first accusations of *hubris* from his supporters, some of whom also grumbled that Alexander was getting dangerously close to going native. Alexander, unphased by these murmurings, journeyed to northern Egypt, where he founded Alexandria in Egypt, his most famous city. After letting his soldiers recuperate and receiving reinforcements, in 331 B.C. he struck eastwards and marched into Mesopotamia, the Persian heartland.

Darius once again marched to oppose him, but Alexander met his forces at Gaugamela and battle was once again joined. Darius had at his disposal anywhere between 100,000 and 250,000 men, while Alexander's force numbered less than 50,000, but once again the relentless machine of the Macedonian phalanx proved its worth by pinning down all of the superior Persian force and resisting all attempts to break through its lines, including attacks by war elephants and scythe-wheeled chariots. Meanwhile, Alexander led his Companion Cavalry and the Macedonian right wing in a flanking movement which outran its enemy pursuit and then struck straight for the center of the Persian formation, against Darius himself. The attack smashed through the Persian lines, causing the Persian center to crumble, and the entire Persian army was routed. Darius fled the field, but Alexander was unable to immediately pursue because his left flank, under general Parmenion, had been pushed back and was in danger of being overrun. This delay allowed Darius to escape, but his defeat was absolute: about 50,000 Persian dead, unknown numbers captured, and the entirety of their baggage train in Alexander's hands. Darius eluded Alexander's pursuit and vanished into the mountainous region of Ectebana (modern Iran). Abandoning his chase to consolidate his territorial gains, Alexander marched into Babylon, where he was acclaimed as a conquering hero. He then marched on Susa, where he captured the Imperial Persian treasury, thus endowing himself and his army with unimaginable wealth. Finally, Alexander advanced towards the royal capital, Persepolis. His way was contested by an enemy army at the Persian gate, but he smashed the enemy force and continued onwards, entering Persepolis in 330 B.C.

While he had entered Babylon peacefully, Alexander decided to make a statement in Persepolis. He allowed his troops to pillage the city for days on end, permitting them to finally take their revenge upon the hated Persian adversaries, and the palace of Xerxes, the famous Persian Emperor who had been defeated at Salamis and Plataea, was put to the torch. It is unclear whether this gesture was a deliberate insult, revenge for Xerxes ordering the burning the Acropolis of Athens, or whether it was the result of one of Alexander's famous drunken binges, but the end result was that the palace and much of the city were reduced to ash.

Alexander was now effectively the ruler of the whole Persian Empire, as well as king of Macedon and *Hegemon* of the League of Corinth besides. All of Asia Minor, the Middle-Eastern seaboard, and Egypt now owed him allegiance, but he wanted more. Prophecies in Jerusalem, Siwa, and Gordium had declared him the future King of Asia, and Alexander wanted to be ruler in name as well as in practice. This could never happen as long as Darius was still alive and still capable of rallying men to his banner, so after letting his army plunder their fill and rest in Persepolis, Alexander marched once more. He chased Darius farther eastwards, from Ectebana into Media, then into Parthia (Western Afghanistan). As Darius's supporters tallied his defeats, they began to slip away.

Eventually, the inevitable happened and Darius, alone and friendless, was deserted by his last troops and taken prisoner by Bessus, one of his generals and governor of Bactria (Central Afghanistan). Bessus kept Darius prisoner for a time as he continued to retreat from Alexander, but when the Macedonian troops threatened to overtake him Bessus had Darius murdered, and his body cast into a ditch. It is likely that Alexander, advancing with the Macedonian vanguard, found Darius dead, but he later claimed that Darius had been alive when he reached him, and had named him his successor. With Darius gone, Alexander could proclaim himself Great King of Persia, but his claim was threatened by a rival: Bessus, having murdered Darius, proclaimed himself Great King in turn and retreated into the heartland of Bactria, defying Alexander to challenge him. Such overt defiance could not be left unpunished: in 330 B.C., Alexander marched into Bactria at the head of his army, to crush Bessus and make himself King.

"To the Strongest"

Factionalism, sloth, and greed had run rampant among many of the governors and other officials of the middle and high levels of Persian infrastructure whom Alexander had wisely chosen to largely leave in their place (rather than substitute them with men who had no idea what their job entailed). Doubtless many of them, when he had marched into Bactria, believed that he would never return, and accusations of bribery and corruption were rife. Thus, Alexander's progress to Susa was marked by a string of executions, as he rapidly made examples of the officials who displeased him. Once he reached the city, Alexander took good care of his beloved veterans: their back pay – which sometimes amounted to several years' worth of salary – was paid in full, with decorations and bonuses for all, and Alexander also promised he would ship injured and old veterans home under General Craterus, one of his ablest commanders. However, this last gesture seems to have been misconstrued by his men: perhaps they thought he wanted to replace the Macedonian units in his army entirely with Persian ones, since Persian youngsters were being taught to fight in the Macedonian phalanx formation. Certainly it cannot be that they did not wish to go home at last, not when they were finally so close.

Whatever their reasons, Alexander's men mutinied once again. For three days they refused to listen to reason, but this time Alexander seems to have greeted their balking with heartbreak rather than rage. It was only after Alexander threatened to appoint some of his Persian subjects to the rank of general and rename Persian regiments with titles properly belonging to old and sacred Macedonian units that his men relented. To show goodwill, Alexander feasted several thousand of his veterans, dining at their tables and making the rounds among them until late into the night. He also attempted to harmonize relationships between Macedonians and Persians by conducting a mass marriage between many of his officers and Persian noblewomen, though to little success. It is around this time that Alexander's closest boyhood friend, Hephaestion, died suddenly under mysterious circumstances, a blow from which Alexander never truly recovered. He grieved Hephaestion for days on end, refusing to leave his quarters.

Busts of Alexander (left) and Hephaestion

It was in action that Alexander found solace. Never a man to sit on his hands or rest upon his laurels, Alexander began planning his future campaigns, which may have included attempts to subdue the Arabian Peninsula or make another incursion into India. But fate had other plans for the young Macedonian king. One night, while feasting his admiral Nearchus, he drank too much and took to bed with a fever. At first, it seemed like the fever was merely a consequence of his excess, and there was not much concern for his health, but when a week had elapsed and there was still no sign of his getting better, his friends and generals began to grow concerned. The fever grew, consuming him to the point that he could barely speak. After two weeks, on June 11th, 323 B.C., Alexander the Great, King of Macedon, *Hegemon* of the League of Corinth, King of Kings, died.

The circumstances of Alexander's death are unclear. Certainly there were plenty of ambitious men, even among his inner circle, who might have wanted him dead, yet all of the main historians for Alexander's life discount the possibility of foul play, claiming no poison was used, and slow-acting venom capable of prolonging a man's agony for two weeks seems technologically unviable for the period in question. Perhaps Alexander was simply exhausted: he was a famous binge drinker, like his father, which did little for his health, and he had been on campaign for more than a decade, having sustained at least three serious wounds in the process. Even today scientists and doctors still try to diagnose Alexander based on accounts of his death, naming potential natural causes like malaria, typhoid fever, or meningitis.

On his deathbed, some historians claim that when he was pressed to name a successor, Alexander muttered that his empire should go "to the strongest". Other sources tell us that he passed his signet ring to his general Perdiccas, thereby naming him successor, but whatever his choices were or may have been, they were ignored. Alexander's generals, all of them with the loyalty of their own corps at their backs, would tear each other apart in a vicious internal struggle that lasted almost half a century before four factions emerged victorious: Macedonia, the Seleukid Empire in the east, the Kingdom of Pergamon in Asia Minor, and the Ptolemaic dynasty in Egypt. During the course of these wars, Alexander's only heir, the posthumously born Alexander IV, was murdered, extinguishing his bloodline for ever. And though it was unclear what killed Alexander, his subordinates were fully aware of the value of his body. According to ancient accounts, Ptolemy eventually took control of Alexander's body, and Alexander's sarcophagus eventually made its way to Alexandria, where it remained for at least the next 500 years.

Bust of Alexander's friend and general, Ptolemy

As the most famous man of history, Alexander's tomb was a must-see for the leaders of antiquity, and apparently his original gold sarcophagus was replaced with a glass casing, allowing his body to ve viewed. Ancient historians wrote some entertaining anecdotes of unknown veracity about certain leaders' visits to Alexander's tomb. Pompey the Great (who took the name Magnus and cut his hair based on Alexander) and Julius Caesar were said to have viewed Alexander's body without causing a stir, but historians claim that when Augustus visited Alexander's tomb, he accidentally knocked Alexander's nose off. And perhaps as a way to emphasize Caligula's insanity, historians claim the young Roman emperor took Alexander's breastplate for his own use. The last known date in which a Roman emperor visited Alexander's tomb was in 200 A.D, but it's unclear what happened to Alexander's body and tomb after that. The location of Alexander's body remains lost to history.

Despite the infighting among them, one thing Alexander's generals did agree upon was their Hellenistic culture. Most famously, Ptolemy's line firmly established the Hellenistic culture of the Greeks while ruling over Egypt. By marrying within their family line, the Ptolemaic pharaohs kept their Hellenistic heritage until the very end of Ptolemy's line, which died with Cleopatra in 30 B.C.

Alexander and his successors also succeeded in "Hellenizing" Persia and parts of Asia Minor, and their influence is still readily visible. Anthropologists have found that some of the earliest Buddha statues constructed in India bear an uncanny resemblance to Ancient Greek depictions of Apollo

This Buddha, with a combined Greco-Buddhist style, dates from the 1st-2nd century A.D.

Further west, much of Alexander's old empire was eventually conquered in the following centuries by Rome, including Cleopatra's Egypt. But instead of ending the Hellenistic culture, the Roman Empire further reinforced it. Having conquered Greece itself around 100 B.C., the Roman Empire heavily assimilated the Greeks' culture into its own. Latin was an offshoot of the Greeks' language, the Romans' mythology was nearly identical, and Roman poetry, literature and art all closely resembled what was produced to their east in the preceding centuries.

Ptolemaic Period

MACEDONIAN AND PTOLEMAIC DYNASTIES

Kings of Dynasty 26 were the first to introduce Greeks to Egypt, brought in as mercenaries to assist Saite against the Persians; Greeks "modernized" the Egyptian army, and introduced new techniques of warfare. Greek merchants also came, they established their own city of Naucratis, and Greek travellers and tourists came to Egypt.

332 B.C., Alexander the Great was welcomed as saving Egypt from the Persians. He had in succession conquered Syria, Palestine, Gaza and entered Egypt without a fight. Tributes previously paid to Persia would now be paid to him. Native Egyptians were permitted to follow their own religious practices (they were suppressed by Persians). There were improved opportunities for trade; he founded coinage; he established cities; he improved education.

Alexander was in Egypt for only six months but he set up systems to convert to Greek methods; Cleomenes of Naucratis was appointed his Viceroy. There were six governors (2 Macedonian with military powers, 2 Greek, 2 Egyptian). Garrisons were established at Pelisium and Memphis, and the Nile fleet was put under control of Macedonians. Alexander travelled as far south as the First Cataract, but built his city as Alexandria (planned as a Greek city), opposite the island of Pharos, at the west side of the mouth of Nile, thus Alexander had two harbors.

Alexander scrupulously paid attention to the Egyptian gods; he sacrificed in the temple of Memphis where he was probably crowned as Pharaoh in the Temple of Ptah. He built a temple at Rhakotes to the mother-goddess Isis.

He also visited the oracle of Jupiter Amun at Siwa Oasis where this god promised him dominion over the whole world. Egyptians interpreted this as Alexander having been given god-like status and therefore his successors could and would be legitimate rulers of Egypt.

In 331 B.C. Alexander left Egypt, and in 323 B.C. he died in Babylon; according to legend he was buried in Memphis, but there is no reliable evidence of this.

Initially, Perdiccas ruled the Macedonian empire as regent for Alexander's half-brother Arrhidaeus, who became Philip III of Macedon, and then he ruled as regent for both Philip III and Alexander's infant son Alexander IV of Macedon, who was born posthumously. Perdiccas appointed Ptolemy, son of Lagos, one of Alexander's closest companions, to be satrap of Egypt. Ptolemy ruled Egypt from 323 B.C., nominally in the name of the joint kings Philip III and Alexander IV. However, as Alexander the Great's empire disintegrated, in 305 B.C. Ptolemy became an independent ruler, designated King Ptolemy I Soter ("Saviour") and founded the Ptolemaic (aka Macedonian) Dynasty. His son was appointed co-regent, the custom of brother-sister marriage was resumed. A "hybrid" god Serapis was created, a mixture of Greek theology with the goddess Osiris.

Ptolemy successfully defended Egypt against an invasion by Perdiccas in 321 B.C., and consolidated his position in Egypt and the surrounding areas during the Wars of the Diadochi (322 B.C.-301 B.C. wars between Alexander's erstwhile generals).

The Ptolemies became Pharaohs in the sense of absolute rulers to whom the taxes devolved, the people were not enriched, there were frequent rebellions, and many Greeks came to live in Egypt, but on the whole Egypt prospered. There became a division (as in Persia) of Hellenistic Greek-speaking cities, and the indigenous population who spoke their own language in the rural areas.

Within a century Greek influence had spread through the country and intermarriage had produced a large Greco-Egyptian educated class. Nevertheless, the Greeks always remained a privileged minority in Ptolemaic Egypt. They lived under Greek law, received a Greek education, were tried in Greek courts, and were citizens of Greek cities, just as they had been in Greece. The Egyptians were rarely admitted to the higher levels of Greek culture, in which most Egyptians were not in any case interested.

All the male rulers of the dynasty took the name "Ptolemy," while princesses and queens preferred the names Cleopatra and Berenice. Ptolemy II married his full sister, Arsinoe II. They became co-rulers, and both took the additional name epithet Philadelphus ("Brother-Loving" and "Sister-Loving"). There is no agreement on whether this followed a prior Egyptian practice, nor whether what would seem to have been incest weakened the next generations in any way. Cult-like state-worship of the ruling dynasty was established. The old Egyptian aristocracy was abolished and replaced by Greeks; a beneficial result of Hellenization was the foundation of the Great Library at Alexandria, the bringing in of scholars from the East, the introduction of processions and Greek style games.

The succeeding Ptolemy pharaohs had to contend with rebellions, and "anti-pharaohs" of Egyptian ethnic origin, before incomplete suppression by Ptolemy V Epiphanes in 186 B.C..

There were military expeditions into neighboring territories, some gains in expanding the empire were made, but at the time of Ptolemy V all were lost, except for Cyprus and Cyrene. The Rosetta Stone commemorates religious ceremonies performed by Ptolemy V.

Dynastic conflicts marred later generations. Ptolemy VIII Euergertes II fought his brother Ptolemy VI Philometor, and briefly seized the throne.

Ptolemy XII Auletes was father to Cleopatra VII, from 51 B.C. they were joint rulers, then she ruled with her brothers to who she was married, Ptolemy XIII and XIV.

The early Ptolemies increased cultivatable land through irrigation and introduced crops such as cotton and better wine-producing grapes. They also increased the availability of luxury goods through foreign trade. They enriched themselves and absorbed Egyptian culture. Ptolemy and his descendants adopted Egyptian royal trappings and added Egypt's religion to their own, worshiping Egyptian gods and building temples to them, and even being mummified and buried in sarcophagi covered with hieroglyphs.

Cleopatra VII Thea Philopator (Cleopatra VII, Goddess, Father-Lover) was born in Alexandria in 69 BC. Her father was the Pharaoh Ptolemy XII Auletes, but because of the incestuous nature of royal marriages in Egypt, it is unclear who her mother was – it appears likely that she was another Cleopatra, Cleopatra V. Like all the Ptolemies, Cleopatra was not Egyptian. Tracing her ancestry back far enough – and indeed, not even that far – demonstrates Cleopatra was descended from minor Macedonian landed nobility and was, in effect, a full-blooded Greek without a drop of Egyptian blood in her. The dynasty to which she belonged had been established by Ptolemy, who took the name Ptolemy I Soter (Savior), a Macedonian general who had been a close childhood friend and then campaign companion to Alexander the Great. Alexander had conquered Egypt while destroying the mighty Persian empire some three centuries before, and after his death, when the wars of the *Diadochii* (the Successors) tore his empire asunder, it was Ptolemy who came to take over Egypt and establish himself there as a ruler. Ptolemy's dynasty had endured ever since, molded in the image of the old Pharaohs that the Persian Empire had long since crushed.

The Ptolemaic dynasty, like the Pharaohs of old, had a tendency to pursue incestuous inter-marriage between brother and sister, though this seems not to have affected Cleopatra in any way – all contemporary sources, whether they disliked her or not, unanimously agree that she was neither deformed or feeble-minded. However, though she suffered no disadvantages due to her birth, the environment she grew up in was hardly the most harmonious for a child. The court of the latter Ptolemies was a veritable snake's nest of plots, deceit, murder and corruption, and never more so than under the reign of the unfortunate Ptolemy XII Auletes, Cleopatra's father. Ptolemy XII's accession to the throne was marked by plotting and bribery on a grand scale, and once he was in place he grew so paranoid that, suspicious of his provincial governors, he insisted on concentrating almost all executive powers in Alexandria, where he had his seat. Such a system of government could not hope to cope with, or indeed understand, the problems faced by the Egyptian kingdom's most farspread provinces, and inevitably there were violent uprisings by those subjects at the borders of the kingdom who felt themselves abandoned to their fate. Cyprus and Cyrenaica were both lost, and other rebellions were crushed only with great difficulty and expense. At this time, Egypt had effectively become a client state of Rome – and a valued trading asset, as they provided the majority of grain imports to the capital – and, in 58 BC, despite unrest at home, Ptolemy was obliged to travel to Rome on an official visit. He chose to take Cleopatra, then just a child, with him as well, but what was meant to be a short trip ended up becoming a three-year exile: taking advantage of his absence, another Cleopatra seized the throne. It is, unfortunately, unclear which Cleopatra this was, exactly. Records from the period are sparse and not helped by the fact that the Ptolemies favored re-using the same names over and over again. She may either have been Cleopatra V, making her Cleopatra VII's mother, or Cleopatra VI, which would mean she was a sister. Either way, this Cleopatra's reign was to be short-lived – within a few months of her accession to the throne, she died suddenly under mysterious circumstances. It is highly likely that she was murdered, most probably at the hand of Berenice IV, Cleopatra VII's older sister, who took the throne as soon as she died. Berenice reigned for just under three years in Alexandria, until Ptolemy XII finally returned, at the head of a Roman army led by General Aulus Gabinius. Ptolemy had been forced to go hat in hand to Rome, having virtually no support outside of Alexandria and no chance of regaining his throne by raising armies of his own. Though this move allowed Ptolemy to recapture the throne of Egypt, he had effectively made his kingdom a vassal state of Rome, garrisoned by Roman armies, propped up by Roman spears, and dependent on Roman goodwill.

Betrayed by at least one of his eldest daughters, if not two (or his wife), Ptolemy seems to have turned to Cleopatra, his companion during his three-year exile, as his sole repository of trust. At age 14, he proclaimed her regent, a largely ceremonial position which nonetheless placed her in direct line to the throne in the event of his death. Ptolemy's reign limped on for another four years, amid further losses of crucial territory and an ever-growing dependence on Gabinius's troops, whose officers had established themselves – apparently permanently – in Egypt and promptly formed their own political faction, the *Gabiniani*, in order to try and carve themselves their own piece of the rich Egyptian pie. Finally, in 51 BC, Ptolemy Auletes died, leaving an 18-year-old Cleopatra at a nonplus. She could not assume sole rulership, for such an act would require her to get rid of her younger brother, Ptolemy XIII, with whom she was expected to share power. Cleopatra was also, in keeping with dynastic tradition, required to marry Ptolemy, who was 10 years old at the time. With the weight of tradition upon her, Cleopatra complied, but her and Ptolemy's was not a happy union. The two seem not to have gotten along as brother and sister, never mind as husband and wife, and matters were not made any easier by the fact that the gods themselves seemed to be conspiring against Cleopatra. Her rule was marked by more uprisings, and to add insult to injury, the Nile stubbornly refused to deliver adequate floods. Egypt's fertile grain fields were dependent on the periodic flooding of the Nile basin, which would coat the fields with a natural fertiliser, but a sparse flood meant even sparser harvests, which meant not only that the people would go hungry but that Egypt would be unable to deliver sufficient grain to Rome, with all the perilous consequences that entailed.

Feeling the strain, just a few months after ascending to the throne, Cleopatra effectively divorced her younger brother, whose influence was limited by reason of his age – she no longer appeared with him at official ceremonies, and started being the sole signatory on official documents, a gross breach of tradition. In Ptolemaic tradition, female co-rulers were technically subordinate to their male counterparts, regardless of whether this was actually the case, so doing away with Ptolemy was a slap in the face to the many traditionalists at court. Cleopatra may have been many things, but she was never anything but brash – perhaps even foolish. Having made enemies of the traditionalists, she promptly followed this political *faux pas* in 50 BC by upsetting one of the most powerful political factions in Egypt, the *Gabiniani*. Having been in Egypt, at a loose end, for approximately five years, the *Gabiniani* had essentially severed their ties to Rome, becoming embroiled in the civil war currently wracking the fledgling Empire in their own right.

When some exponents of the *Gabiniani* murdered the sons of Marcus Bibulus, the governor of Syria, who had been sent in friendship to request their aid in a military campaign against the neighbouring Parthians, Cleopatra saw a chance to intervene and cut the *Gabiniani* down to size. She had the assassins seized, put in chains, and delivered to Bibulus, but while this may have curried favour with the Roman governor, it did nothing to endear her to the *Gabiniani*, who promptly went from uneasy allies to sworn enemies. Cleopatra could hardly hope to rule long in the face of such massed political hostility, and in 48 BC, a plot spearheaded by Pothinus, a eunuch in the palace service, with the collusion of Cleopatra's many enemies, forced her from the throne and placed the more biddable, pliant Ptolemy XIII on it as sole ruler of Egypt. Cleopatra was a fugitive.

Civil War

Cleopatra Appears before Caesar, by Leon Jerome

Cleopatra did not take her exile lying down. She immediately attempted to raise the province of Persilium against her brother, but faced with lack of support, she was forced to flee deep into the interior. Ptolemy sent troops to apprehend her, but the teenaged ruler had other, bigger fish to fry.

Rome, Egypt's *de facto* overlord, was in the process of tearing herself apart, and the repercussions of this conflict were being felt across the Mediterranean. Gaius Julius Caesar, former consul and governor of Gaul, had marched across the Rubicon, illegally bringing his armies onto Italian soil and threatening Rome herself, with the purpose of making himself dictator. Caesar was opposed by his former ally, the once-great general Pompey Magnus, but Pompey was an old, spent man while Caesar was still vigorous, and Caesar had chased Pompey's army from Rome, hounded it all the way to southern Italy, and then, when Pompey escaped across the Mediterranean to Greece, he had loaded his army onto a fleet and shipped it across the sea, where he had annihilated Pompey's armies at Pharsalus in 48 BC. Pompey had barely escaped with his life, and virtually alone and penniless, he had taken ship for Egypt, where he arrived as a supplicant, possibly hoping for military assistance from the *Gabiniani*, or from Ptolemy himself.

Having heard a rumor that Pompey was attempting to raise men against him in Egypt, Caesar took ship for Alexandria, only to find upon his arrival that Pompey had been murdered on the orders of Egypt's young pharaoh, the boy-king Ptolemy XIII. Possibly encouraged by Pothinus, Ptolemy had Pompey Magnus put to death almost immediately after his arrival in Egypt, the end result apparently being that he hoped to ingratiate himself with Caesar, whose victory at Pharsalus had, by default, made him the uncontested ruler of Rome and thus the most powerful man in the known world.

Ptolemy, however, had completely, monumentally misunderstood Caesar. When the Roman general arrived in Egypt a bare two days later, hot on Pompey Magnus's heels, Ptolemy received Caesar with great pomp and presented him with Pompey's head. He could not have insulted Caesar more, or rendered him more furious, if he had slapped him in the face. Pompey had been a close friend of Caesar's before their rivalry spiralled out of control, and had even married Caesar's daughter, who had died in childbirth before the war.

Utterly enraged by what he referred to as Ptolemy's casual barbarism, Caesar asserted Rome's superiority over Egypt – not to mention the fact he had an army on Egyptian soil – by installing himself in Alexandria and proclaiming himself arbiter of the dispute between Cleopatra and Ptolemy. All of this quickly reached Cleopatra, who had plenty of spies in the Egyptian court, and she realised that Ptolemy's colossal blunder was a heaven-sent chance to reassert her claim to the Egyptian throne. Already fairly certain that Caesar's new-found loathing for Ptolemy would lead him to side with her in any case, Cleopatra decided to strike while the iron was hot.

She quickly travelled to Alexandria, where Caesar had taken up residence in Ptolemy's palace. At a loss as to how to actually enter the palace itself, which was heavily patrolled by Ptolemy's personal guard in addition to Caesar's own men, she finally settled upon an idea which has fascinated the world ever since. She had one of her followers, Apollodorus the Sicilian, wrap her into a carpet, hoist her onto his shoulder, and march her past the palace guards.

When Apollodorus was received by Caesar, he unrolled the carpet and Cleopatra, slightly dishevelled but otherwise none the worse for wear, appeared before the Roman general. Caesar was 52 at the time, just over three decades older than Cleopatra, who was 21, but Cleopatra might well have known that Caesar was something of a womaniser, having already conducted a famous affair with Servilia, the mother of Marcus Brutus. Be that as it may, Cleopatra chose to appear before Caesar virtually *en desabilhee*, wearing little to nothing, and most of the sources from the ancient world agree that the Egyptian queen was a famous beauty. She seduced him, by all accounts, that very night, and it seems the ever ambitious Roman eventually came away impressed by the lavish and exotic lifestyles Egypt's royalty enjoyed.

It is unclear whether Cleopatra ever truly loved Caesar – that is something that only she can ever have truly known – but she was certainly canny enough to realise the political advantages of a liaison with him. Prior to Caesar and Cleopatra's meeting, all evidence pointed to Caesar intending to do away with Egyptian independence altogether, and formally annex Egypt into the Roman dominion. However, after they began their relationship in such a spectacular fashion, Caesar promptly discarded his annexation plans and became the principal backer of Cleopatra's claim to the throne of Egypt.

Ptolemy was not prepared to take Cleopatra's sudden ascendancy lying down, however. Shortly after Caesar made his formal announcement of support for Cleopatra's claim he fled the city with most of his entourage, and raised his armies. Caesar, who had only 4,000 men with him, could not hope to fight, so for almost a year between 48 and 47 BC he and Cleopatra were besieged inside a compound within Alexandria's walls. However, the besieging force was unable to breach the compound and seems to have contented itself with attempting to starve Caesar and Cleopatra out, something which was impossible as they were able to keep their lines of communication open and resupply themselves via fortified access to the sea, which the compound possessed. In January of 47 BC, Caesar managed to get word to Mithridates of Pergamum – an ancient rival of Egypt, ever since the wars of the *Diadochii* – and request his aid. Mithridates marched with some 16,000 men, causing Ptolemy's forces to fall back. Caesar sallied from Alexandria, combined his forces with Mithridates, and marched upon Ptolemy's army.

The two armies, both around 20,000 strong, met at the Nile shortly afterwards. Caesar's veterans, the shock troops, were in the vanguard and they attacked the Egyptian troops, which were equipped as a traditional Macedonian Phalanx with heavy bronze armour, shields, and 18-

foot pikes. Roman armament and tactics were superior to the Phalanx, something they had already amply proved in their conquest of Greece, and Caesar's men and their allies made short work of Ptolemy's force, instigating a rout. Ptolemy himself was caught in the headlong, panicked rush for safety, and he drowned attempting to cross the Nile. With his death, Cleopatra became *de facto* sole ruler of Egypt, with Caesar's blessing, though for formality's sake she married Ptolemy XIV, another brother, to appease the traditionalists at court. Caesar chose to linger in Alexandria for a further three months, despite his presence being urgently required in Rome. During this time, Cleopatra also gave birth to a boy, whom she named Ptolemy "Caesarion" Caesar, who she claimed to her dying day was Caesar's son, though Caesar himself steadfastly refused to formally acknowledge the boy as his.

Having ended the Egyptian civil war in Alexandria, Caesar was ready to return to Rome, which was about to be introduced to Egypt's young queen. At this point in his life, Caesar had been married to Calpurnia, who he had taken as a wife in 59 B.C., but having extramarital relationships was hardly abnormal for a powerful Roman at the time.The following year, in 46 BC, Cleopatra visited Caesar in Rome, where he was in the process of having himself proclaimed dictator for life, much to the chagrin of his opponents in the Senate. Her visit provoked something of a scandal; foreign mistresses were all very well, and it was accepted that a Roman general might warm his bed any which way he chose when he was away from home, and heads would be politely turned the other way. It was quite another matter, however, for Caesar to openly flaunt his mistress before all and sundry, and especially before his long-suffering wife, Calpurnia, who retired into seclusion over the matter.

Several of Caesar's enemies, most notably the famous orator Cicero, were outspoken in their disgust for Caesar's relationship with the Egyptian queen, but Caesar appears not to have cared – possibly as a consequence of his growing arrogance. He appeared publicly arm in arm with Cleopatra on a number of formal occasions, and commissioned a gold-lacquered statue of Cleopatra, depicting her as the Egyptian goddess Isis, to be placed in the temple of Venus Genetrix he had personally endowed. He was canny enough, however, not to give in to Cleopatra's repeated insistences that he make Caesarion his heir, something he could not theoretically do, in any case, since Cleopatra was not a Roman citizen. Cleopatra was desperate for her son to be proclaimed Caesar's successor, but in the event Caesar chose to appoint his nephew, Gaius Octavian, as his heir, with a provision that if Octavian should die before him then his inheritance should pass to Marcus Brutus, his former lover Servilia's son. In the next two years, Cleopatra was often in Rome, alternating her time between there and Alexandria which, thanks to Caesar's intervention and diplomacy, was finally stable enough to allow her to leave the city for months at a time. Most of the factions who had plotted against her had been crushed, and with no other pretenders to the throne and the biddable Ptolemy XIV as her co-ruler, Cleopatra was reasonably satisfied. Barring the matter of Caesarion's succession, she could not have been happier.

The bliss was not to last. On the Ides of March in 44 BC, Caesar was murdered by a mob of Senators on the floor of the Senate House, victim of a plot orchestrated chiefly by his would-be-heir, Marcus Brutus. When Caesar entered the Senate House, he was approached, as arranged, by a *Liberator* named Tillius Cimber, who presented him with a petition for the cancellation of the exile of his brother, who had been banished some time previously. Caesar ignored him and brushed roughly past, but Cimber seized hold of his robe, half-pulling his toga from him. Caesar snatched his toga away from Cimber, demanding "What is this violence?". It was at this point that Servilius Casca, who despite his confession to Antony had decided to go along with the plot after all – doubtless in fear of what the other *Liberatores* would do to him if he got cold feet – attacked. He also seized Caesar by his robe and, drawing his dagger, dealt the Dictator a glancing cut to the neck. Casca was no assassin, and the cut seems to have been trivial, so much so that Caesar, who had doubtless seen worse on campaign, turned and seized him by the neck, snarling "What are you doing, you wretch?". Casca panicked and, dropping his dagger, screamed "Help me, brothers!". His desperate entreaty broke the paralysis that had seized his fellow *Liberatores*, with upwards of 60 men descending upon Caesar. The Senators were not military men, which was made clear by the haphazard manner in which they stabbed Caesar with knives and daggers. Caesar, stabbed multiple times, tripped and fell to the ground, where the conspirators continued to savage him. Despite the fact Caesar was stabbed nearly two dozen times, doctors concluded only one of them was a fatal wound.

It has been suggested that it was Servilia who, jealous of Cleopatra, planted the idea of a plot into her son's head, though it will never be possible to know the whole truth of the matter. Cleopatra, who was in Rome at the time, was forced to flee for her life. She took shelter in Alexandria, devastated by Caesar's death, and secluded herself in mourning.

Cleopatra, as shown in a contemporary Egyptian statue.

The End of the Ptolemies

Following Caesar's death, aside from her desire for vengeance, Cleopatra's first instinct seems to have been to protect her son Caesarion, and ensure his future. Caesar had died without naming Caesarion heir, or indeed even formally recognising him as a son and Roman citizen, and his position in Egypt was also far from secure. As the well-publicized bastard of a Roman, he could not hope to inherit Cleopatra's crown, so Cleopatra had to act.

Just a few months after Caesar was brutally slain in the Senate House, Cleopatra quietly did away with Ptolemy XIV (it has never been proven that she was behind his sudden death, but family tradition suggests that when a Ptolemy becomes fatally indisposed, his closest relatives usually have a hand in the matter), and Cleopatra formally raised Caesarion to the title of co-regent and successor, since at that point there were no more male Ptolemies to take the throne in his stead. Having firmly established Caesarion as her heir, Cleopatra could turn her eye to foreign affairs: Rome was once again in the process of tearing herself apart, with Brutus and Cassius, the chief plotters involved in Caesar's death, on the one side, and Octavian (Caesar's heir) and Mark Antony, a veteran of Caesar's Gaulish, Italian and Greek campaigns and dashing hero of the Roman mob, on the other. There were two distinct factions vying for supremacy, as there had been when her brother Ptolemy had fatally made the choice that cost him his throne and his life – the question was, could Cleopatra choose any more wisely?

Antony

Cleopatra was faced with the first great crisis of her reign since Caesar had first disposed of Ptolemy XIII and placed her upon the throne, and she reacted with her customary impulsiveness, although her decision was almost certainly a foolish one. Brutus and Cassius, following an incident in the aftermath of Caesar's death when Mark Antony's oratory had incensed the Roman mob into howling for their blood, had fled Italy with the legions loyal to them and taken refuge in Asia Minor, where they had set about carving out a power-base for themselves, with remarkable success. Their position, so perilously close to Egyptian territory, meant that they directly threatened Cleopatra's throne, particularly as the ever-fickle Nile had once again delivered unsatisfactory floods, meaning that Egypt was wracked by famine, and the army severely weakened.

However, Cleopatra would never agree to ally herself with Egypt's enemies. Instead, she sent aid to Publius Dolabella, a prominent supporter of Caesar's who had aligned himself with Antony and Octavian and who also held a power-base in the East. Dolabella was hardly a match for Brutus and Cassius, though, and in 43 BC his forces were surrounded and destroyed, with Dolabella himself committing suicide to avoid capture and the dishonor of defeat, in the traditional patrician manner. Cassius was furious at Cleopatra's defiance, and realizing Egypt's extremely vulnerable position, he quickly outfitted an army with the intention of invading Egypt, removing her forcibly from the throne, and annexing her territory to the former conspirators' eastern domains. However, even as the expedition was about to set out in autumn of 43 BC, Cleopatra was – unwittingly – saved at the eleventh hour by Brutus, who recalled Cassius and his army to Smyrna, where he needed reinforcements against the forces of Antony and Octavian.

Despite the recall, Cassius was not prepared to have Cleopatra's troops come to Antony and Octavian's aid, so he left one of his crack generals, Lucius Murcius, in command of a veteran legion and a fleet of approximately 60 ships, with which Murcius garrisoned a cape on the southern tip of Greece, knowing Cleopatra's fleet must pass nearby if she was to reinforce the Caesarians. Cleopatra, either because she was unaware of Murcius' ambush or because she trusted that she could defeat him, embarked her army onto her fleet and sailed nevertheless, but adverse weather proved to be her downfall. The Mediterranean is a treacherous sea to this day, especially in winter, and Cleopatra's fleet was smashed and scattered by a violent storm which lasted for days, causing Cleopatra herself, who had insisted on accompanying the expedition, to become violently sick. The remnants of her ships turned tail and limped back for Alexandria, while to the east, Murcius had to fight nothing but the wreckage of several of her galleys, which washed up on the shore he was patrolling.

Cleopatra's forces were fatally weakened, and she herself for a time was bedridden and too ill to attend to affairs of state. If Brutus and Cassius had been victorious, doubtless Egypt would have been made short work of. In the event, however, later in 42 BC, the armies of the two former conspirators were destroyed by Mark Antony and Octavian at Philippi, in Northen Greece. This victory effectively destroyed Brutus and Cassius, leaving Octavian, Antony and their ally Lepidus in control of Rome, having established Rome's second triumvirate (the first having been Caesar, Pompey, and Crassus).

Octavian was given Rome and the West, Lepidus Africa and Iberia, and Antony himself took the east as his personal domain. Accordingly, in 41 BC he summoned Cleopatra to his seat in Tarsus. It appears that Cleopatra had been accused of paying a massive bribe to Cassius to ensure the safeguarding of Egypt, which had allowed him to levy more troops and pay more mercenaries to oppose the Caesarians. Whether the accusations were true is a matter of debate, but either way Antony wanted to have words with Cleopatra personally, in order to test her loyalty. Another reason for the meeting was that Antony intended to wage war against the Parthians, Rome's age-old enemy in the East, and to do so he needed the logistic and financial support of Egypt. Perhaps he simply wanted to meet the famous beauty who had so completely seduced his old friend Caesar for himself.

Be it as it may, Cleopatra presented herself before him at Tarsus in the winter of 41 BC, arriving with all the pomp and circumstance that a queen of Egypt could summon. Like Caesar before him, Antony fell for her – or was seduced by her – almost on sight. Once again, it is unclear – as we will see from her later actions – whether Cleopatra truly loved Antony, or was just using him for his power. Perhaps the question is not so cut-and-dried, and she was doing a bit of both. Antony himself was so captivated by her that he chose to spend the remainder of the winter and the spring of 40 BC in Alexandria with her, exciting scandal in Rome not just as a consequence of their liaison – Cleopatra had been the mistress of Antony's closest friend, after all, and Antony had a wife, the Roman aristocrat Fulvia – but because, taking advantage of Antony's power in the east, Cleopatra had her sister Arsinoe murdered. Arsinoe, who was Cleopatra's one surviving sibling, was likely more than familiar enough with her other siblings' fates, and as the last one standing she had taken refuge at the temple of Artemis, in Ephesus (Greece), which was under Antony's jurisdiction. Arsinoe claimed the right of sanctuary, but that hardly stopped Antony's henchmen, who dragged her onto the temple steps and butchered her, thus removing once and for all the last credible threat to Cleopatra's throne. This elicited great scandal in Rome, where the right of sanctuary was held to be sacred, and Octavian, who was at odds with Antony, wasted no chance to use the story to discredit him.

In late spring of 40 BC, Antony abruptly cut his relationship with Cleopatra short. Whether he feared the relationship would utterly condemn him in the eyes of the mob, or he felt guilty over the predicament of his wife Fulvia, who despite the rumors concerning him and Cleopatra's liaison – or possibly disbelieving them – was steadfastly campaigning on his behalf against Octavian, is unclear. What is certain, however, is that the relationship between Antony and Cleopatra, however brief, had been intense. Nine months later, Cleopatra gave birth to twins, Alexander Helios and Cleopatra Selene, who could only be Antony's children. Quite what Cleopatra made of Antony's abandonment, however, is unclear. In all likelihood, she was fairly confident he would be back – he had a war against Parthia to prosecute, after all, for which Egypt would be an ideal base, and her seat in Alexandria was the wealthiest city in Antony's new domain.

Antony set out for Rome, but while he was on his way there he received news that his wife, Fulvia, had died prematurely while still steadfastly opposing Octavian's political smear campaign against him. Seeing a chance to patch things up with Octavian, Antony agreed he would remarry, to seal the alliance that would keep the crumbling triumvirate alive, at least for a time. Accordingly, later that year he married Octavian's own younger sister, Octavia Minor, as Pompey Magnus had once married Caesar's daughter, to preserve the unity of the first triumvirate. Cleopatra must have been less than thrilled at this union, especially as she was heavily pregnant with Antony's twins, to which she gave birth two months later, but Antony had his plate full ensuring support for his cause at home, and with the ever troublesome Parthians.

It was at this time that the Parthians, apparently sensing weakness, advanced eastwards, conquering large swathes of Syria and Judaea, which were essentially Antony's backyard. Capitalizing on the renewed goodwill engendered by his marriage with Octavia, Antony convinced his fellow triumvir Octavian to provide him with an army and sufficient supplies, and set off for Parthia to drive the enemy's forces from his domains and then, if all went well, to march into the Parthian heartland itself. However, Antony detoured to Greece on his way, where he scandalized Roman public opinion by proclaiming himself the incarnation of the god Dionysus, displaying a foreshadowing of the penchant for gluttony which would come to haunt his and Cleopatra's final days. Meanwhile, Octavian had re-routed the army he had promised Antony to Sicily, where a rebellion by one of Pompey Magnus's sons was underway. Despite attempts by Octavia to patch things up between her husband and her brother, in 38 BC Antony decided that Octavian would never truly support his Parthian venture and so, in disgust, he abandoned his wife and children in Rome and set sail for Alexandria.

It appears that Cleopatra took her erstwhile lover's return in stride, and there appears to be no doubt that the couple happily reunited. With her trademark impulsiveness, Cleopatra pledged Antony the money he needed to fund his Parthian expedition from the Egyptian royal treasury, and Antony married Cleopatra, according to Egyptian customs, later that year – Octavia's presence in Rome being conveniently forgotten. Antony then left Cleopatra behind and marched to war, achieving some notable initial successes in Judaea in 37 BC, where he installed Herod on the throne. He then marched on Parthia, but his campaign proved to be a catastrophe. A full quarter of his 100,000-man army was lost to disease, desertion and battle, and Antony was unsuccessful in subduing either Parthia or Armenia, being forced instead to limp back to Cleopatra with his tail between his legs.

While Antony struggled in the east, back in Rome Octavian had dismissed Lepidus, the third member of the Second Triumvirate, and assumed sole power over his domains, while also continuing a vigorous smear campaign against Antony, denouncing him for abandoning Octavia and his children and accusing him of having gone native with his wanton Egyptian queen. Octavian's public relations offensive blamed Antony's recent failure and the consequent loss of Roman life on the wrath of the gods for Antony's sins.

Antony and Cleopatra, however, seem to have been unconcerned with Octavian's threats, or the growing popular resentment with Antony that Octavian was fomenting in Rome. It seems quite likely that Antony simply did not care any more and just wanted to be left alone in his Alexandrian idyll with the woman he loved. Like Caesar, Antony was fully charmed by the quixotic and exotic Egyptian lifestyle, and he immersed himself in it even more than his famous mentor. Despite repeated demands from Octavian that he return to Rome immediately to answer for his ill-conduct, Antony remained happily in Alexandria, and waged a new campaign against the Armenians in 34 BC, this time achieving success and annexing the territory to his and Cleopatra's domains.

It was in the aftermath of this war that Cleopatra and Antony finally overstepped their mark. Cleopatra organised a lavish, Roman-style Triumph in Alexandria to mark Antony's successful conquest, during which Antony's children (now numbering three) by Cleopatra were all granted royal titles in the East, Cleopatra herself was named Queen of Queens and ruler of the East, and crucially, Cleopatra's son Caesarion was named King of Kings, ruler of Egypt and the East, living God, and above all – Caesar's formal sole son and heir, thereby by default disowning Octavian in the eyes of the East. Additionally, Antony officially declared his alliance with

Octavian over, proclaiming that from then on the East was free and independent of Rome. It was the worst blunder of Cleopatra's life.

Between 33 and 32 BC, relationships between Rome and Alexandria steadily broke down. In Egypt, Antony and Cleopatra accused Octavian of not being Caesar's true heir, pointing out that Caesarion was Caesar's actual son, not his nephew, and thus the worthier man to bear his name – a dangerous statement for Octavian, whose main source of public support, especially with the legions, was their love for his deceased adoptive father. Antony also unilaterally divorced Octavia, disowned his children by her, and threatened to stop the grain supply to Rome, while Octavian demanded Antony answer for waging war on Parthia and Judaea without the Senate's consent. Utilizing public relations yet again, Octavian made accusations of outright treason, while infuriating the Roman mob with tales of the excesses that the no-longer-Roman Antony indulged in within Cleopatra's palace.

In 32 BC, Octavian declared war against Cleopatra, rather than Antony, a calculated move intended to ensure the Romans did not feel he was continuing the legacy of the fratricidal civil war. Perhaps Octavian overestimated his support, for Cleopatra and Antony were delighted to discover that both consuls and a full third of the Senate had decamped from Rome and defected to their side wholesale. The royal couple met the defectors in Greece, and for a while felt so secure in their position they even considered an invasion of Italy itself.

Their victory was to prove short-lived, however. In 31 BC, Octavian's forces set sail for Greece, and the legions there immediately went over to his side, spurred by the veterans in their ranks who had once fought for his adoptive father Caesar. Both Cyrenaica and Greece fell to Octavian, essentially without a blow struck, and Cleopatra and Antony were forced to retreat back to Egypt, where they rallied the Eastern navies and prepared to contest Octavian's passage across the Mediterranean.

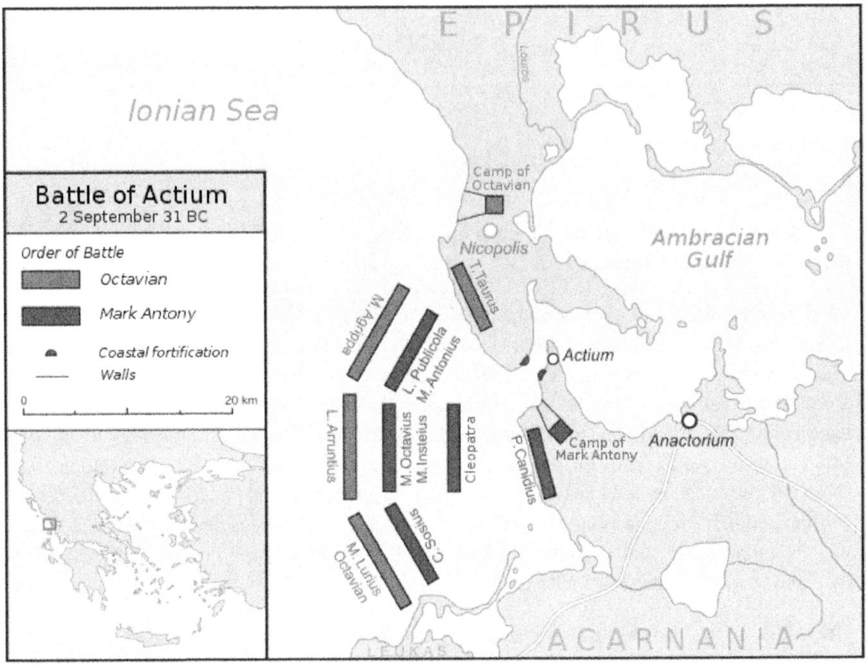

On September 2, 31 BC, Antony and Cleopatra found themselves in a tactically disadvantageous position, facing Octavian's navies off the coast of Actium, in Greece. With the risk of being bottled up and surrounded at Actium by Octavian's naval forces a very real possibility, Cleopatra advised Antony to give battle, although it appears the Roman general thought victory was an unlikely possibility. Antony and Cleopatra appeared, to the untrained eye, to have the advantage: their fleet numbered over 500 vessels, almost half of which were giant five-decked quinquiremes, ramming warships that carried full-blown siege engines on board, while Octavian had only 250 far lighter craft.

However, the sea was rough that morning, favoring Octavian's more maneuverable ships, which were less affected by the rolling swells, and to make matters worse, Antony's fleet had been wracked by disease, meaning that many of his mighty quinquiremes were undermanned. The giant craft were ponderous to begin with, but without the requisite number of rowers and fighting men, they could never hope to achieve proper ramming speed. Octavian's lighter, more agile craft, filled with veteran sailors, were able to dance around the ponderous quinquiremes, showering them with hails of fire arrows, ramming and boarding where they could, and sprinting away before the heavier craft had a chance to bring their rams to bear. As the day wore on, it became more and more apparent to Antony and Cleopatra, on their twin flagships, that the battle would be lost. More and more of their craft were being sunk, scattered or overwhelmed, and still more were burning down to the waterline, their skeleton crews being insufficient to man their battle stations and extinguish fires at the same time. As night approached, Antony and Cleopatra spotted a gap in the now thoroughly jumbled enemy line, and ordered their ships to speed through it without delay, making for Alexandria with all speed and abandoning their entire navy to its fate. It was a crushing blow, for Octavian and his generals had virtually annihilated Egypt's seaborne power.

As one of Rome's most famous battles, and one of the most famous events in Cleopatra's life, the Battle of Actium has taken on a life of its own in popular memory. One of the longest-held myths about the battle is that Cleopatra, sensing defeat, began to sail away from the fight in the middle of the day, and the lovestruck Antony followed her with his own ship, abandoning his men in the middle of the fight. While that popular myth would be in keeping with explaining Cleopatra's irresistible charm and magnetism, contemporary accounts of the battle do not suggest it was actually the case.

Actium was the decisive battle in the civil war between Antony and Octavian, but Antony and Cleopatra's troubles were far from over. They retreated to Alexandria, and Antony was still fairly certain he could give Octavian a run for his money on land – he was a famous, veteran commander, after all, and he had at his disposal 19 legions of infantry and more than 10,000 cavalry. However, due to a combination of disgust over his callous abandonment of his navy at Actium, a strong sense of loyalty to Caesar and his heir Octavian (and a healthy dose of common sense, in all likelihood), in August Antony's army deserted *en masse* and went over to Octavian virtually to the last man, leaving Antony and Cleopatra stranded in Alexandria, with just their personal bodyguard for defence, at the mercy of Octavian. Antony, furious at his army's betrayal, flew into a rage and raved against Cleopatra, declaring that she had betrayed him to Octavian in hopes of saving herself. Cleopatra was so terrified for her life that she locked herself away in her private rooms, and sent a message to Antony saying that, because she believed all hope was lost, she had taken her own life.

It remains unclear whether this was a callous act, deliberately engineered to drive Antony to commit suicide himself, or if Cleopatra was genuinely distraught and not thinking clearly. Whatever the case, Antony was so overwrought that he could see no other recourse than doing what any true, noble Roman would do in the event of his defeat - fall upon his sword. He made a botch of the job, however, giving himself a deep but non-fatal wound to the stomach. He laid himself down upon a couch, hoping that blood loss would carry him off, but as the blood flow slowed and the wound grew ever more painful, he began to beg for the release of death. Hearing of his plight, Cleopatra was horrified at what she had done, and commanded he be brought to her. Even in in his death throes, Antony was so happy to hear that she was alive that he consented, even though this required his being winched through a window, as Cleopatra had barricaded herself in her quarters. He died shortly thereafter, in her arms.

Cleopatra was so distraught over the note which had caused Antony to suffer such a painful and drawn-out death that she tore her clothes off, ripping at her hair and beating and scratching herself in her despair, before managing to achieve a measure of composure. She was captured by Octavian while praying over Antony's corpse, but though she was placed in the care of trusted men, Cleopatra would not suffer the final indignity of being paraded through the streets of Rome before the howling mob. As everyone now knows, Cleopatra famously took her own life.

Of course, the manner of Cleopatra's death has been debated for millennia, shaped in popular memory by everyone from Shakespeare to Hollywood. Ancient historians wrote that she had a venomous snake, most likely a cobra, concealed in her private apartments, and that when she realised that escape was impossible, she provoked it into administering a fatal bite on her arm. Today most people unfamiliar with those accounts believe that Cleopatra had an asp bite her on the breast, which was how Shakespeare depicted it in his famous play. Stories differ as to what snake was used (the term "asp" is most likely a generic name for any venomous snake, but Egypt is renowned for its deadly King Cobra) and if it was kept deliberately or came to be there by accident. Some historians even argue that there was no snake at all, and that Cleopatra poisoned herself with hemlock, as Socrates had done. Still others claim Octavian had her killed, which seems contrary to the widely-assumed belief that Octavian intended to parade her as a captive through the streets of Rome in a triumph.

***The Death of Cleopatra* by Reginald Arthur, 1892**

Thus died Cleopatra VII, Thea Philopator, the last of the Ptolemies. Her line, which had lasted approximately three centuries, was extinguished with her. Her son Caesarion was almost certainly murdered soon after her death on the orders of Octavian, as all trace of him mysteriously disappears from the historical record, so the dynasty that Alexander's general had founded in the wars of the *Diadochii* came to an abrupt end.

Despite her own personal successes, Cleopatra's legacy was a ruinous one: her line extinguished, and her once independent (if subservient) kingdom reduced to a province governed directly from Rome. She had become mistress, in turn, to two of the most powerful men in the world, loved them in her own unique fashion, but betrayed one of them – Antony – in his gravest moment of peril. She was ruthless, strong-willed, arrogant in many respects, foolish in a great many others, and her political and military career, once she stepped out of the confines of Egypt, was a fiasco. Yet she was a remarkable woman for all that – anyone who has herself smuggled in a carpet past her rival's guards in order to snatch a crown from their fingers deserves admiration. Beautiful, reckless, cruel, and wanton – she was everything her enemies in Rome decried her as, but she was also ambitious, loyal, headstrong, and in many ways, wise beyond her years. Not the perfect woman, perhaps, but a great one.

Roman Egypt

The function of Egypt was to provide grain for Rome. Governing systems of the Ptolemies remained unchanged with the same officials, but Roman law was introduced. Greeks continued to staff most of the administrative offices and Greek remained the language of government except at the highest levels. Unlike the Greeks, the Romans did not settle in Egypt in large numbers. Culture, education and civic life largely remained Greek throughout the Roman period. The Romans, like the Ptolemies, respected and protected Egyptian religion and customs.

The country flourished with the stability of Rome, but Rome reaped all the benefits, not the native Egyptians. Augustus continued the tradition of temple building and made offerings to Apis-bull, and in Nubia Cornelius Gallus led expeditions and more temples were built.

Augustus respected Alexander and left Alexandria intact. He added a racetrack and amphitheater, and a Caesareum (started by Cleopatra), and employed for cult worship of the Caesars.

Several subsequent Roman emperors visited Egypt. Hadrian (A.D. 117-138) traveled more extensively than any others in A.D. 130, but his male lover, Antinous, sacrificed himself by drowning in the Nile to fulfil the prophecy that Hadrian would have a great loss, thereby saving him from a worse one; Antinoupolis is named in his memory.

Christians in Egypt

A.D. 50, Decius ordered persecution of Christians in Alexandria, but Constantine I (son of Saint Helena) ended the persecution. In A.D. 311 with an Edict of Toleration and the Edict of Milan in A.D. 313, he restored their property to them.

When Constantine founded his eastern empire based on Constantinople, it became the recipient of Egyptian grain.

The Caesareum of Alexandria was converted to a church dedicated to Saint Michael, and the seat for the Patriarch of Alexandria. Egypt became a diocese of Rome, divided into six provinces.

Even at Thebes an altar was dedicated to Constantine.

Theodosius I by Edict declared Christianity as the state religion in A.D. 384 and all temples dedicated to the old gods were closed but were not destroyed.

Modern Egypt

The Origins of Modern Egypt

1798: Napoleon Bonaparte invades Egypt

Egypt was in disarray, and Napoleon thought a relatively easy victory over the English could be obtained by occupying Egypt and setting it up as a stopping point on the way to the ultimate goal of India. He proposed to the *Directoire* that such an invasion would not only embarrass England but would also support the interests of French trade. From a personal point of view, Napoleon could imagine himself following in the footsteps of Alexander the Great. The *Directoire* agreed to his plan, in part to rid themselves of Napoleon's presence, a threat to their own authority.

Bonaparte Before the Sphinx, by Jean-Léon Gérôme, 1868

A major armada was assembled in the Mediterranean ports under French control: 40,000 soldiers, 10,000 sailors, 13 ships of the line, 14 frigates and 400 transport ships. They sailed May 19th 1798, and on June 9th took Malta from the Knights of the Order of Saint John, who capitulated rather than fight an impossible battle.

Napoleon landed at Alexandria on July 1st, 1798, and defeated the Egyptian forces at the Battle of Subra Khit and then again, two weeks later, at the famous Battle of the Pyramids, where modern European infantry tactics – most notably the square formation – proved to be completely invulnerable to attacks by unsupported Egyptian cavalry. French losses were less than 30, while the Egyptians lost 2,000 men killed, further cementing Napoleon's status in the minds of his troops as an invincible general. The British Mediterranean fleet had been sighted, and after the soldiers had all disembarked, the French fleet withdrew from Alexandria to seek a better defensive position in Abukir Bay.

Napoleon's transport ships returned to France, while the battleships remained in Abukir Bay where Nelson and the British fleet found them 1st of August. Nelson split his ships, one section to each side of the French Fleet, between land and French ships as well as the open water. The battle lasted a few hours and the French fleet was totally destroyed, with only four of the 17 ships able to escape. Napoleon recognized he had lost his means of leaving Egypt and set about establishing himself in place as the ruler.

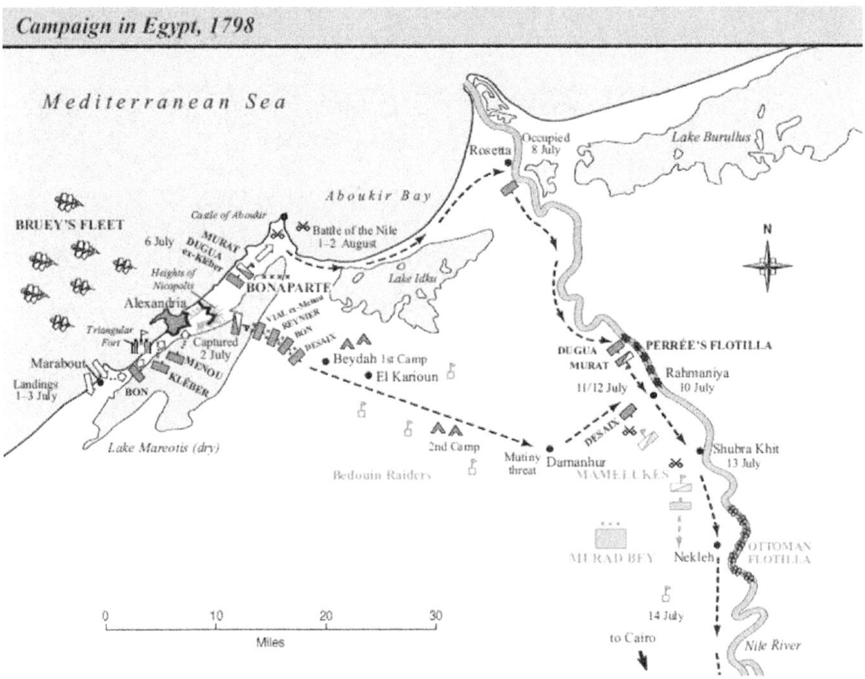

Napoleon made declarations of friendship, good intentions, and respect for religion; pilgrims travelling to Mecca were protected. A governing body, *diwan*, of local notables was set up, French civilising institutions were created: libraries, health services, museums and a zoo, dictionaries were made, newspapers founded.

His army, greatly diminished by disease as well as combat fatalities, was reinforced by 3000 sailors who no longer had ships, and they were needed to cope with the uprisings, starting with some slight ones before a major rebellion broke out on 22nd October 1798. This was suppressed with some difficulty and many French deaths; ultimately the rebels took refuge in the Great Mosque expecting a degree of mercy, but after shelling the mosque, the French soldiers broke in and killed all who were there. The *diwan* was abrogated, and replaced by French military rule. Many executions of suspected leaders followed the destruction of the mosque.

Napoleon also set about exploring the region for his own interests. He explored the Canal of the Pharaohs, the predecessor of the Suez Canal.

1799: Ottoman Response

Believing Napoleon was severely weakened by the British naval defeat, the Ottoman rulers mounted a campaign to displace him from their territory of Egypt. A two pronged attack was planned, by land from Syria and by sea from Rhodes, but Napoleon, when he heard the plan, pre-empted the land attack by marching his own troops into Palestine and capturing Arish in two days. He then moved on to the port of Jaffa, where in the early days of March his cannon destroyed the defences. The French soldiers were turned loose in the town, following the custom of the day when a town resisted rather than surrender. Following the precedent set by Richard Lion Heart at Acre, Napoleon murdered 4,000 prisoners rather than leave them behind to fight another day.

Plague began to visit his army at this time, with further loss of soldiers he could ill afford. He followed Richard's progress in reverse, going north up the Palestine coast, and like the early Crusaders found himself blocked by the defences of Acre. He had additional support from siege guns brought by sea, and since Ottoman reinforcements were on the way, he had to finalize the capture of Acre. Napoleon nearly achieved it, having entered the fortifications, but remarkably he was opposed by a fellow military academy graduate now fighting for the Ottomans, by crews from British ships, and the Ottoman garrison of Acre. In May he quit the assault.

The retreat from Acre is not as well known as the retreat from Moscow, but must have been as pitiful. At first the wounded and plague sick were carried, then they found this too much of a burden, so they killed their own men. All horses were given over for transport, and everyone walked, Napoleon among them. A scorched earth policy was executed, everything was destroyed in the wake of the army. By the time they reached Egypt, they had lost 1800 soldiers, two thirds to battle, one third to plague, and had as many wounded who managed to walk to Egypt. Those wounded who did not have the good fortune of dying were captured by the Ottomans, who tortured and beheaded them.

July 1799: Battle of Abukir and Napoleon's Departure

The Ottomans landed a substantial army and had reinforced their defensive positions at Abukir, but despite the pitiful state of his army, Napoleon went immediately on the offensive. It was estimated 10,000 Ottoman soldiers were drowned in their retreat, the remainder were otherwise neutralised; the leaders were captured and brought to Cairo as a triumphal Roman style procession of prisoners to laud Napoleon the victor.

In August, recognising the hopelessness of his position, Napoleon slipped away at night and with his three ships reached France without British interference. General Kléber reached an agreement with the Ottomans, the Convention of al-Arish, which was to allow the French soldiers to withdraw, but the British would not permit them to do so without surrendering. Kléber was assassinated, and his successor, General Menou, married an Egyptian woman, converted to Islam, and was comfortable in Egypt. He developed plans to improve industry and agriculture, plans that clearly would have to be supported by increasing taxes, and they came to nothing.

March 1801: An Anglo-Ottoman force occupied the Nile Delta. After a small amount of fighting the French concluded they had had enough, they capitulated to the British at the end of August 1801 and were repatriated to France in British ships.

From the campaign the British gained the Rosetta Stone and many antiques accumulated by Napoleon, while the French lost 30,000 soldiers. The Treaty of Paris in 1802 ended all hostilities between France and the Ottoman Empire.

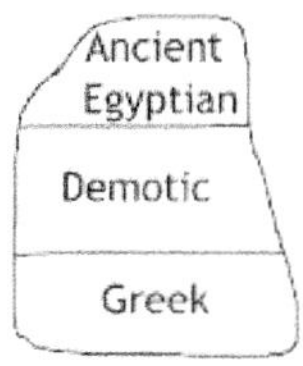

Rosetta Stone and key

What did Egypt get from the French Invasion?

To Egypt in particular, and to the Muslim world in general, the superiority of western armies was painfully demonstrated. But from a cultural point of view, Egypt was brought into contact with French liberal thought and technology, and it also inherited the Napoleonic code of laws.

1801-1802: First British Occupation Of Egypt

The British had for the greater part been involved in sea battles around Egypt, notably the Bay of Abukir, but they did eventually land soldiers who in conjunction with Ottoman troops wiped up what remained of Napoleon's army before shipping the survivors home.

Under the 1802 Treaty of Amiens, British forces agreed to leave Egypt.

Restored Ottoman Suzerainty, 1801-1914

Mehmet Ali: The Founder of Modern Egypt

1805: Mehmet Ali (aka Muhammad; Mehmed; in Albania as Mehmet Ali Pasha; in Turkish as Kavalalı Mehmet Ali Paşa)

Mehmet Ali was of Albanian stock, born 1769 in Rumeli (which is today part of Greece). He came to Egypt in 1801, leader of a 300 man contingent of Albanian soldiers, as part of the force landed to oust the French invaders. To him is attributed the first of the internal actions to modernize Egypt, and from him was descended a long line of rulers.

During the first four years Mehmet and his Albanian soldiers remained in Egypt, there was an uncertain leadership in the region due to disputes between the *ulema* religious leaders, the remaining Mamluks, and Ottoman civil servants. Mehmet Ali entered into politics without showing his hand too clearly, but enough that in 1805 there was a clamor for the governor (*Wali*) to step down and be replaced by Mehmet, a decision to which the Sultan Selim III had to agree in March 1806.

The Mamluks were professional soldiers whose only interest was in being a warrior caste; originally of slave origin from the Caucasus, they had become a dominant force in the Ottoman Empire, and after the French left they conspired against all other civil authority. After Napoleon's departure and the British evacuation, they were still the feudal owners of Egypt, and their land was still the source of wealth and power.

Mamluk warrior

On March 1st 1811, Muhammad Ali invited all of the leading Mamluks to his palace to celebrate the declaration of war against the Wahhabis in Arabia, bringing between 600 and 700 Mamluks to parade in Cairo. Near the Al-Azab gates, in a narrow road, Ali's forces ambushed and killed almost all of them in what came to be known as the Massacre of the Citadel. During the following week, hundreds of Mamluks were killed throughout Egypt, and the death toll for Mamluks and their relatives throughout Egypt was estimated at 3,000.

Mehmet Ali's Reforms of Egypt

a) Nationalization of land: All Egypt was "nationalized." In this way the state owned all of the land, achieved by putting such high taxes on the tax collectors they had to capitulate and allow the land to be taken by the state. The government would decree what use the land would be put to, would allocate seeds, tools, fertilizer, control irrigation etc.

Cash crops were expanded from the traditional wheat to indigo, tobacco and cotton. The work was harder, but the pay was better, more labor was required and families increased in size commensurately, doubling the population.

French engineers were employed to create or improve the system of canals for irrigation, permitting three crops a year for each section of land.

b) All trade was conducted through the state; the state then sold on the commodities; as a result the farmers' income increased 400%, and "long staple" cotton thrived (an industry of importance to be discussed later).

c) Industry was aimed essentially at improving the capacity of the armed forces, but attention was given also to the needs for transportation – barge canals, river ports and roads were constructed. For agriculture, mechanisms were developed for weighing and storing grain, for refining sugar, for spinning cotton. The factories in Cairo made hand weapons, muskets and cannons. The shipyard in Alexandria began to build a navy.

The downside of this: factories need laborers; weapons need soldiers. Europeans were introduced as managers and teachers of industrial arts, peasants were drafted by a system of corvée labor to work in factories, to build the canals, to make the roads and to serve in the military.

Initially this was resented, machinery was sabotaged, but little by little an urban factory class developed, the work became better paid, and from them sprang the generation of professional classes, the doctors, lawyers, engineers and teachers.

d) Administration of government had been in the hands of the Mamluk class who had been eliminated; Mehmet Ali had to create a whole new class of bureaucrats. He divided Egypt into 10 provinces, and to a large part each was run by a member of his family.

e) The military had to be reformed, and this was accomplished in part by sending young officers to Europe, in particular France, for a military education, and then to rewrite military manuals in Arabic.

f) Education was promoted away from the usual schools which taught only the Koran to schools that taught the traditional broad range of subjects known in Europe, once again French was pre-eminent.

Military expeditions

Mehmet Ali was first and foremost a soldier, and his initial loyalties were to his employer, the Sultan of the Ottoman Empire, but only initially. The Saud family had moved from central Arabia to capture the holy cities of Medina and Mecca, and with that they began to enforce their Wahhabi doctrine. In 1803 Mehmet Ali conducted a campaign into Arabia and took the land from the control of the Saudis (who returned after World War I and took it back again). In the meanwhile, Hejaz came under Ottoman rule, reinforced by further campaigns conducted by his son Tusun, in 1811 and 1812. One campaign against the Saudis resulted in the capture and execution of Abdullah ibn Saud, the clan chief.

British Alexandria expedition of 1807

This was an attempt by the British to take Alexandria as a Mediterranean port to further the war against the French and the Ottoman Empire, with whom the French had now formed an alliance. 5,000 soldiers were landed, commanded by General Alexander Mackenzie-Fraser, and very little resistance was met until they advanced into Rosetta, where hidden snipers caused serious casualties and the British withdrew. In continuing action led by Mehmet Ali, some British were taken prisoner and were marched through a parade of their 900 dead comrades' heads mounted on sticks, but the live prisoners were not poorly treated.

Negotiations were held on a reasonably amicable basis, prisoners were released, and the British forces withdrew in ignominy.

Other Campaigns

Other campaigns led by Ali's numerous sons were conducted south of Egypt into the Sudan, Ethiopia and Uganda.

In 1821 the Greeks rebelled against the Ottoman rulers, and Mehmet Ali was asked to participate in suppressing the rebellion with Crete as the reward. Ali sent another son with 16,000 soldiers, 100 transports, and 63 escort vessels. Unfortunately for him, Greece had the European powers on their side, and on 20th October 1827 the entire Egyptian navy was sunk.

Despite that debacle, Mehmet Ali bounced back. A new navy was built, and a new army was recruited, trained and equipped. In October 1831 he was ready to pursue his dream of conquest of the Levant, which included part of modern day Israel, Lebanon and Syria. They would give him a skilled trading population, natural resources and trade routes; they would also bring him close to Anatolia, the mainland of the Ottoman Empire. An excuse for making war is generally de rigeur, and Mehmet Ali claimed Syria was sheltering Egyptians who were evading their civil or military obligations.

With that pretext, Ali won Syria easily in 1831, although Acre which only surrendered after a siege that lasted to May 1832. Ali then went on to enter Anatolia and defeat the Ottoman army at Konya in December 1832. The potential that he might take control of the entire Ottoman Empire greatly alarmed the Western powers who preferred the *status quo*, and in May 1833 the Convention of Kutahya required Mehmet Ali to withdraw from Anatolia and receive Crete (as the Sultan had first promised) and Hejaz (central Arabia) as compensation.

Mehmet Ali's end game

In 1831 Mehmet Ali advised the Western powers he would declare Egypt to be an independent country. The West was not pleased, and the Sultan resisted with military force, but his soldiers entered Syria and were soundly defeated at the Battle of Nezib in June 1839. Salt was rubbed into the wounds when their navy defected to join with Ali's.

When the Western powers ordered Ali to withdraw, he hesitated, and in response British and other European warships took up position on the Nile. In September 1840, they began shelling Beirut, and in November Ali reluctantly agreed to a severe reduction of his army and navy and to give up Crete and the Hejaz. As a compensation, he was granted hereditary rights as ruler in Egypt and the Sudan. Thus, Egypt became an autonomous province, but still within the Ottoman Empire.

By the time it was all said and done, the over-expenditure on military prowess left Egypt deeply in debt, to the tune of 2.5 million pounds sterling. Senility gradually overtook Ali, who ceased to rule in 1848 and died the following year.

Though Mehmet Ali is widely considered the founder of the modern Egyptian State, he never intended that Egypt would be ruled either by or for Egyptians. It was to be the "family business." As a result of his defeats of the Ottoman rulers, however, Europeans began to think of Egypt as an autonomous state.

After Mehmet Ali

1848, July-November: Ibrahim Pasha, acting governor

Ibrahim was Mehmet Ali's oldest son, and he assumed the power of *Wali* when his father was beyond the task by virtue of his mental deterioration. He had already demonstrated his capacity as a leader in military expeditions, but he ended up pre-deceasing his father.

1848-1854: Abbas Hilmi I, governor

Son of Tusun, the next oldest male family member, and grandson of Mehmet Ali, Abbas became Regent of Egypt after his uncle Ibrahim died in November 1848, and then officially became the *Wali* when his mentally incompetent grandfather died in August 1849.

His reign was a mixture of undoing some of Mehmet Ali's progressive changes and supporting others. He discharged many of the long time advisers who had been used to doing things the French way. He undid trade monopoly agreements, reduced taxes, gave land away from state control, handed over factories to private enterprise, and reduced the size of the army (which was crippling the treasury).

One of his most important reversals of his grandfather's policies was to permit Egypt to become a transit point between the Mediterranean and the Indian Ocean by building a railway between Alexandria and Cairo in 1851. This shortened the four month trip around South Africa to India to six weeks. He also accepted an officer of the British Peninsular and Orient Shipping Line to produce in 1850 a detailed project for a canal.

Abbas' life ended July 1854 when he was murdered by his own palace guard.

1854-1863: Muhammad Said Pasha, Governor

The practice in inheritance of position was to appoint the oldest male member of the family, which explains why Abbas Hilmi, Muhammad Said's nephew, preceded him. Said, a son of Mehmet Ali, was appointed *Wali* after Abbas was murdered.

Unlike his brothers who had largely been concerned in military adventures, Said was educated in France, and among his friends was Ferdinand de Lesseps, who resigned his position in the French diplomatic corps and came to Egypt when Said unexpectedly came to power.

Ferdinand de Lesseps

Suez Canal

It had been well established long ago that there was no significant difference in the level of the Mediterranean Sea and the Red Sea, and that a canal between the two was feasible. Linant de Bellefonds, chief engineer of Egypt's Public Works, had made plans for a canal across the Suez isthmus, but Mehmet Ali wanted no part of it. Numerous other experts had tried to do the same, but Britain for some reason was opposed and preferred the Alexandria to Cairo railway which was built by Stephenson.

As his personal friend, though he was not an engineer, Ferdinand de Lesseps obtained from Said the right to form a company that would dig the canal, but international cooperation was required in the contract of the "Commission Internationale pour le percement de l'isthme des Suez." After extensive surveys, the Commission produced its report in December 1856. The British were opposed and the government dissuaded English investment, which impeded raising the anticipated cost of $40 million. Nevertheless the "Compagnie Universelle du Canal Maritime de Suez" was formed in December 1858 and work began April 1859.

It was de Lesseps friendship with Said that made the canal possible. When land was needed, Said saw it was made available. When labor was required to dig the canal by hand, 20,000 workmen a year, Said saw that forced (corvée) labor was made available without being too concerned about anti-slavery laws in force. When de Lesseps was out of funds, his friend Said chipped in with the purchase of more of the company's shares. When the Ottoman government interfered with the use of slave labor, Said produced Egyptian government funds for industrial excavation equipment. De Lesseps was belatedly required to "treat the natives well – they are men", and with that worker conditions improved. The British, ever willing to criticise the French, made official complaints about slave labor, to which de Lesseps responded by pointing out the British had been a lot less particular when they were building their railway.

The Suez Canal would open after 10 years of construction in 1869.

Reforms

Said followed a program of encouraging European investment and participation in Egyptian life, and many from the professional classes settled in Alexandria and Cairo, with the resulting European style housing present today. An objectionable side effect were the "capitulations", which exempted foreigners from the rule of Egyptian law and obligations to pay taxes, and encouraged a less than desirable expat community development.

Egyptians were given the opportunity to buy land and a middle class developed. The Sudan benefited by the official banning of slave raiding, but unofficially this still occurred.

In 1854 Said established the Bank of Egypt as the country was going into debt, partly as a result of the support of the Suez Canal; by 1863 the foreign debt was $30 million.

Cotton

The American Southern States of the Confederacy depended on "King Cotton" for their economic well-being. An idea was devised that if they failed to ship cotton to England, a large part of whose workforce were dependent on the manufacture of cotton goods, then England would be forced to join in the Civil War on the side of the Confederate States. So they introduced an embargo on themselves; cotton was stored in the warehouses and bonds were sold, much as a commodity market is operated today. However, as the South hoped to harm England's economy in particular, the British had managed to stockpile plenty of reserve cotton, and ultimately the effect of the South's ban was to create a greater demand for cotton grown elsewhere. During the American Civil War, the demand for Egyptian cotton boomed, introducing a false sense of hope into the economy. Egypt incurred debt, but when the American Civil War ended, the demand for Egyptian cotton fell off even as the foreign debt remained.

1863-1879: Khedive Ismail

Son of Ibrahim, grandson of Mehmet Ali, educated in Europe, fluent in French; all of this made Ismail seem a good candidate for the job. When he inherited the post of *Wali,* Egypt was doing very nicely with its trade in raw cotton, thanks to the American Civil War, and that was his downfall. It's hard not to draw a parallel with the easy money that led to a 21st century building boom in parts of Europe, and the easy seduction of bankers offering money.

After he returned to Egypt he was given a number of responsible diplomatic tasks, including a mission to the Pope, to the Emperor of France (Napoleon III), and to the Ottoman Sultan. He was given the military responsibility in 1861 of leading an expedition into the Sudan to suppress an uprising.

Khedive of Egypt

Khedive is a term of Persian origin and approximately equal to "prince." It is a title of more significance than *Wali,* and it was at first refused by the Sultan but later granted in 1867. Ismail also obtained from the Sultan decrees (*firman*) that inheritance of title would be from father to son (no longer the oldest male), and a grant of virtual independence of Egypt from the Ottoman rule. Needless to say, these came at a price. Egypt would also have the right to float loans without first obtaining Ottoman permission, and that created its own price.

Reforms

Some of the changes he made:

Bureaucracy: remodelled the customs system and the post office; established an assembly of delegates in November 1866, though anticipated as an advisory body and not executive.

Education: school systems were improved.

Communications: telegraph lines were erected.

Culture: Egyptian Museum, National Library, Geographical Society, opera (commissioned Aida) and a theater, landscape gardens in major cities.

Industry: stimulated commercial progress, created a sugar refining industry, improved cotton trade.

Edifices: built palaces, greatly expanded Cairo, building a new quarter modelled on Paris, and Alexandria was also improved.

Transportation: He launched a vast railroad building project in Egypt and Sudan; canals were dug, bridges were built.

Social changes: reduced slave trading and extended Egypt's rule in Africa.

Geographic changes: In 1874 he annexed Darfur, but was prevented from expanding into Ethiopia after his army was repeatedly defeated.

War with Ethiopia

Ismail had delusions of empire building to encompass the entire region of the Nile, down into its source in Abyssinia (Ethiopia) and the western borders of the Red Sea. He believed also that Abyssinia was fertile land that would feed the increasing population of Egypt.

He did succeed initially in establishing territorial gains, accepting grants of territorial control from the Ottoman Empire in 1865, and by 1872 he had established huge cotton plantations in territory stretching to the Red Sea. But all his dreams came to an end with military defeat in 1876 by the Abyssinian army. In 1884 with the Anglo-Egyptian-Ethiopian Hewett Treaty, the land he had taken was surrendered (only to be seized by Italians in 1890 and designated Eritrea).

Suez Canal

The canal started by his predecessor, was officially opened by Said to great acclaim and presence of royalty in November 1869. It had (of course!) cost twice the original estimate. The first commercial ship to use the canal was the British P&O *Delta*, and although the British government had done all they could to obstruct the canal, the P&O suggested it long before it became a fact.

Still, the canal was not an immediate financial success, and deeply in debt Isma'il Pasha was obliged in 1875 to sell his shares for £4,000,000 to the United Kingdom.

Debts

Just as in the 21st century, the Faustian bankers and the major European powers had loaned money to Egypt at the height of the cotton boom, now falling away after the Civil War concluded, and they wanted their money back. Ismail had expended it on the Suez Canal, on his buildings and railways, and on his war with Ethiopia. The national debt had climbed from 3 million to 100 million pounds sterling – and there was no money. He sold his shares in the Suez Canal for 4 million pounds, and that barely touched the debt.

A Public Debt Commission was established in 1876, and the Khedive agreed to a Commission composed of representatives of the governments of Britain, France, Italy and Austria to investigate his financial obligations. Following further loss of finances related to low water levels on the Nile and the Russo-Turkish war, the Khedive submitted his finances to joint French-British "Dual Financial Control": they would collect the taxes and control government expenditure. The Khedive humiliated himself by adding English and French Ministers to his cabinet, and appointing an Armenian as Premier. In 1878 he turned over his personal estates to the nation, and accepted he was now a mere constitutional sovereign.

It was at this point he made his declaration, "My country is no longer in Africa; we are now part of Europe. It is therefore natural for us to abandon our former ways and to adopt a new system adapted to our social conditions." It may well have had a bitter twist to it. Although the larger cities had developed distinct European flavors, most Egyptians lived in poverty, were illiterate, and suffered hard labor and heavy taxation.

Nationalist Resistance

The debt commissioners did at the end of the 19th century what the Spanish and Greek governments are doing at the start of the 21st century. They cut expenditure on public works, education and the military, they delayed payments on everything, and of 2,600 officers, 1,600 were to be retired. Street demonstrations quickly followed.

Khedive Ismail resumed control and ordered the soldiers back to barracks, sent the European ministers home, and appointed a new cabinet with his son, Prince Tawfiq at its head, and a competent though westernized minister, Sharif, to draw up a new constitution. Pay cuts were rescinded, but the debt remained.

France proposed a military occupation of Egypt, which Britain opposed, not because "it wasn't nice" but because they wanted no other power between England and India, and France had just been beaten by Prussia. Germany demanded the Ottoman Sultan should depose Ismail and replace him with Tawfiq.

Ismail received telegrams from the Sultan in Istanbul, addressing him as "ex-Khedive," and informing him there was no further need for his services. Two days later he was on his way to Naples.

1879-1892: Khedive Tawfiq

Tawfiq was Khedive Isamail's oldest son, and he led an unremarkable life without any public office until he was appointed in 1878 to be head of the cabinet council when Ismail was forced into the position of constitutional sovereign. He was quite unprepared for office when his father was deposed.

The new khedive was so displeased by the news of his accession that he struck the servant who first brought the tidings to him. Egypt and Sudan at that time were involved in financial and political troubles brought about by the policy of Ismail, and the situation was made worse by the inaction of Britain and France for some months following Tewfik's accession. He found general disaffection throughout the now impoverished country, and he knew and saw no way to alter that.

In November 1879, the "Dual Control" was re-established, but the Egyptian cabinet no longer had any foreign ministers. In 1880 the Commission was taking 50% of the nation's taxes to repay debts to foreign interests, with consequent slashing of budgets for all public services. The foreign expats, which included Turks and Circassians, who were living in Cairo and Alexandria, continued to be exempt from taxation

Urabi revolution

January 1881, Colonel Ahmad Urabi led a delegation of officers to Prime Minister Riyad. The War Minister planned to arrest them, but this was pre-empted by their soldiers storming the building to rescue their officers. Better conditions were promised for the military and the War

Minister was replaced.

In September there was a further threat against Urabi, but in a face-off with the Khedive Tawfiq backed down, the cabinet was dismissed, a new constitution was to be written, and all the retired officers were called back to duty with the army.

Colonel Urabi

For the first time, the new constitution gave executive power to the legislative assembly. Urabi was a national hero, but the expat community was concerned about the rise in military power, and European governments began to threaten occupation. The Egyptians were not dismayed and became assertive, and in response Britain and France sent warships.

However, the Ottomans had lost large areas of their territory in the war with Russia and were not open to losing more to European countries. In June 1882 there were riots in Alexandria, which were suppressed by the army at a cost of 3,000 Egyptian lives, including 50 expats killed or wounded. The British ordered the Egyptians to dismantle the defensive works at Alexandria, seized their tardiness as an excuse and shelled the city, while the French ships withdrew. Alexandria was on fire, and the English landed to extinguish it.

Tel-el-Kebir and aftermath

The Egyptian cabinet meeting in Cairo declared war on Britain, but the British fleet entered the Suez Canal, landed soldiers at Ismailia and on September 10th 1882 fought an indecisive engagement at Kassassin. On September 13, the British under General Wolsey confronted the Egyptian army under Colonel Urabi at Tel-el-Kebir. Knowing the Egyptians would be asleep at night, General Wolsey ordered an unusual frontal assault at night, beginning at 5:45 a.m. before daybreak. The Egyptians were taken by surprise, the battle was finished by 7:00 a.m., and the losses were 57 British and 2,000 Egyptians. The British cavalry now rode towards an undefended city of Cairo.

Urabi surrendered, Wolseley arrived in Cairo by train, Khedive Tawfiq was reinstated, Urabi was exiled to Ceylon, and the British were firmly in charge. From that time forward the British took control of the Egyptian army, trained according to British standards and commanded by British officers.

Sudan

While the British were wondering what to do with their army in Egypt, the *mahdi* ("rightly guided one", a soubriquet adopted by Muhammad Ahmad) revolted against Egypt, and a British force sent to relieve Khartoum was ambushed. Still, the British decided it was not yet the time to withdraw their army.

In November 1882, the British abolished the Dual Control, and Lord Dufferin was sent out to report on the dire financial straits of Egypt, on which claims were now being made for destruction of property in Alexandria, and the costs of support of the British occupation. The army was virtually shut down, public expenditure was slashed and schools were closed.

Making matters worse, in 1883 a cholera epidemic broke out, and here the Khedive came into his own, going with his wife to Alexandria to visit and encourage the sick in the hospitals.

In 1884, Sir Evelyn Baring (later Lord Cromer) was sent to Egypt as diplomatic agent and Consul-General of Britain; he had previously served as one of the debt commissioners and was more than familiar with the problem; he was to remain in Egypt for the next 24 years. Baring sought to improve Egypt fiscally by improving the lot of the peasantry, the bulk of the population. This he thought could be achieved by reduction in taxation on sheep, goats, grain weighing and salt, reduction of forced labor, and improvement in irrigation. British engineers worked to improve existing systems since there was no money for new ones, and with their assistance there followed improved irrigation and a dramatic rise in agricultural production. In five years the tide against national bankruptcy was turned.

Baring encouraged Tewfik to show his activity in administration of his country, and he showed a genuine desire to govern Egypt for its own benefit. He accepted the importance to Egypt of British assistance and support, and he held himself aloof from any palace intrigue.

Meanwhile, the war in the Sudan was not going well, Gordon and thousands of Egyptian troops were killed by the rebels, known to Kipling and the British Tommies as "fuzzy-wuzzys", and the British pulled out of the Sudan. They were contemplating pulling their army out of Egypt altogether, on the proviso they would re-enter if a revolution required it; however, since French conspirators whispered that meant they would come back when and how they wished, the end result was they didn't leave at all.

1892-1914: Abbas Hilmi II, khedive

Suddenly and unexpectedly, Tewfiq died in his Helwan Palace, close to Cairo, on 7th January 1892. His oldest son, Abbas, succeeded him.

Abbas as a youth had been taught by British tutors in Egypt, but he was a 17 year old student at an Austrian military academy when he unexpectedly inherited the position of Khedive. By manipulation of calendar differences between the Muslim lunar months and the Christian Gregorian system, it was calculated he had reached his 18th birthday, and was therefore not in need of a Regent. With that, there was no official reason for Ottoman interference in British interests in Egypt.

From the outset, Abbas had difficulty grasping that he was not free to do as he wished, that Egypt was under British control, and that he was obliged to work with them. It was suggested that the difference in age between Abbas and Baring had something to do with this, and Abbas may have resented the "fatherly" attitude, equally it is probable as a young man newly come to power he did not realize its limits. In January 1893, Abbas appointed a nationalist as prime minister, forcing the pro-British prime minister (Mustafa Fahmi) out of office. Baring called for more troops to be sent from Britain, and to resolve matters Abbas and Baring compromised with a third candidate, veteran politician Riyad.

There was another *faux pas* when Abbas criticized British led units of his own army. When Kitchener offered his resignation, Baring (now Lord Cromer) through Prime Minister Riyad required a public apology from Abbas, which was resentfully given. Abbas was learning his place the hard way.

Britain's military position in Egypt

The British military presence had been reduced from 20,000 to 5,000, but there was no legal basis to justify their presence, no matter how slight the number. There was no agreement with the Ottomans, nor Egypt, nor international treaty to justify their continued occupation of Egypt. The khedive, however, understood they were his support against rebellions, and the population at large was indifferent. Still, some nationalist movements were afoot in the late 19th century, usually comprised of the educated classes who had been taught by Europeans, and who "worked with words" as lawyers, journalists and teachers themselves. They wanted the foreign occupying troops to leave their country.

Society for Revival of the Nation

Mustafa Kemil

Mustafa Kemil as a student had led anti-British protest marches. He chose the French law school in Cairo, in part because Egypt had inherited the Napoleonic code of laws since the time of the French invasion, and the British had never seen reason to change them. He went to France to continue his studies in Toulouse, and was host to a banquet celebrating the Sultan's accession day, secretly funded by the khedive.

Unsurprisingly, his anti-British sentiment found support in France, but also from Constantinople. Back in Egypt, he founded the secret "Society for the Revival of the Nation" with the khedive as a leading member, which later became the National Party. He was not inclined to armed rebellion, he played with pan-Islamism which European countries universally feared, and as Abbas aged, matured, and came to accept the English assistance to his country, Kemil and Abbas went their separate ways. He died from tuberculosis at the age of 33, his funeral procession drew mass crowds, and he had left his mark.

As Egypt's debt diminished, as the country became more prosperous, European investment returned and a larger class of expats developed. As in British India, when the wives came a gulf was established between the "natives" and the Europeans, with their own clubs and societies into which the Egyptians had no right of entry. Resentment mounted. The British, although they assisted in the development of agriculture, were not interested in assisting industry which might compete with factories in Britain, so Egypt was to produce raw goods such as cotton but not be permitted to weave it. Schooling was kept at a low level, and English was to replace Arabic as more suitable for understanding science.

Taba Affair

The British regarded Sinai as part of Egypt, a useful buffer between Ottoman held Syria and the Suez Canal. Abbas gave control of the eastern shore of the Gulf of Aquaba to the Ottomans while retaining the western shore, but the Ottomans encroached on this by building a fort at Taba to the west side. British gunboats in the Gulf persuaded them otherwise.

Gulf of Aqaba

The surprising reaction of Egyptian nationalists was against their own country's interests and in favor of the Ottomans, because they thought the British were only looking after British interests and Istanbul was their real protector.

Denshawai Incident

Another affair in June 1906 typified the arrogance of the British officer and the helpless attitude of the Egyptians who had no choice but to tolerate them. Some officers on a shooting party entered a village with the intention of shooting pigeons, and in response the villagers explained they liked their pigeons and the pigeon manure in the barns was valuable. The British shot at them anyway, starting a barnfire. As the villagers tried to disarm the officers, a gun was discharged probably by accident and a village woman was wounded and four others struck with birdshot. The officers panicked, two ran away, and one was overcome with heat stroke and died. The rescuing soldiers thought the peasant who was supporting the dying officer was responsible and beat him to death.

The colonial powers would not leave well enough alone. The next day, 52 villagers were arrested, a summary trial convicted them of murdering the officer who had died of heat stroke, and four were sentenced to death by public hanging. Others were sentenced to penal servitude for life, terms of hard labour and public flogging. All of this despite the evidence of the Egyptian police official who accompanied the soldiers to the village and testified that after the woman had been shot, the officers fired twice more into the mob. He was sentenced to two years imprisonment and 50 lashes for his intransigence.

There was widespread disapproval, as much by liberal Englishmen as by nationalist Egyptians, which did much to strengthen the hand of the Nationalist Party. After the death of Mustafa Kemil, the party split between a number of leaders with diverging views. To control them, the government in 1909 required newspapers to be licenced, but ways around this, some taking advantage of Capitation laws, were found by those protesting British rule.

Sir Eldon Gorst and Lord Kitchener

As he aged, Abbas became more accepting of the British presence, and in their turn the British began to loosen the reins. In 1900 Abbas paid a second visit to Britain, during which he said he thought the British had done good work in Egypt and declared himself ready to cooperate with the British officials administering Egypt and Sudan. His relations with Cromer's successor, Sir Eldon Gorst, were excellent, and they co-operated in appointing the cabinets and in checking the power of the Nationalist Party.

However, when the Prime Minister was murdered by a young member of a secret society bent on mass extermination of those who collaborated with the British, there was further inhibition of transfer of powers to the Egyptians. Moreover, Gorst, struck with cancer, resigned in 1811.

The appointment of Kitchener to succeed Gorst displeased Abbas, and relations between him and the British deteriorated. Kitchener often complained about "that wicked little Khedive" and wanted to depose him. He took a strong stand against nationalists but was genuinely interested in improving the lot of the peasantry and in representative government.

When the Ottoman Empire joined the Central Powers in World War I, the United Kingdom declared protectorate status over Egypt on 18th December 1914, deposed Abbas, and replaced him with his uncle, Hussein Kamil. Hussein died in 1917 and was followed by Fuad.

By then, the British took over Egypt completely, using it as the base from which to launch military attacks into Ottoman occupied Syria. The country was swamped with British and Dominion soldiery who behaved like soldiers always do. The agriculture was changed to growing wheat, animals were commandeered, and young men were conscripted to be auxiliary troops. All of this contributed to growth in nationalist, anti-British, feeling.

Ambiguous Independence, 1918-1945

Britain took Egypt for granted, and after the war, when moves were afoot to break up the Ottoman empire, no thought was given to Egypt. Representatives of Arabs, Jews and Armenians were invited to the peace conference, but Egypt was not.

The Egyptians thought to send a *wafd* (delegation) and the name of Saad Zaghlul was prominent. He had a history of arrest for belonging to a nationalist movement, then went to France to study law, and after returning to Egypt to practice law was made a judge. His career was also helped by friendship with a princess, his marriage to the Prime Minister's daughter, and the friendship of Lord Cromer.

Saad Zaghlul

Saad became Minister for Justice in 1910 but quit over differences two years later; when Kitchener made arrangements for a Legislative Assembly in 1913 he was successful as a candidate and in January 1914 was appointed Vice President of the Assembly. However, the

Assembly was suspended at the outbreak of war, never to meet again.

The Assembly was replaced by an unofficial Wafd party, on whose behalf at the end of the war Zaghlul met with the British High Commissioner, Sir Reginald Wingate (older cousin of Orde whom he influenced), to enquire in regard to Egyptian independence. They were brushed off by the Foreign Office, and after Prime Minister Rushdi resigned no one would take the office. The Wafd received 100,000 signatures in support, unrest mounted, and with that the British exiled Zaghlul to Malta.

In response to Zaghlul's exile, a major uprising took force. Students went on strike, shops were looted, railroad tracks blown up, telegraph wires cut; and rioters were killed or injured. To show the ecumenical nature of the protests, Coptic priests appeared in the mosques and Muslim preachers stood in the pulpits. The army and the police quelled the riots, but General Allenby, the new High Commissioner, sensibly ordered the return of Zaghlul from Malta.

The British appointed Lord Milner to negotiate in 1920 in London with Saad Zaghlul, and a prospective document of quasi-independence was offered. However, Saad Zaghlul would not accept it, and the British government rejected it.

Britain's Declaration of Independence for Egypt

Allenby persuaded the British government to advise Sultan Fuad they would negotiate with a delegation of his picking, and Fuad selected Adli Yakan. However, when the negotiations collapsed, Saad (who now represented the "spirit of national dignity") was exiled once more, leading to further strikes and riots.

Once again, Allenby's good sense and sympathetic judgement prevailed. After discussions in London, he returned at the end of February 1922 with a formal statement ending Britain's protectorate and declaring Egypt to be a quasi-sovereign state: there were clauses regarding provisions for communications and war, and there were 200,000 foreigners in Egypt who ran most everything that mattered, including the army. The foreigners continued to be protected from Egyptian law by the Capitulation treaty, meaning Egypt did not have total sovereignty.

Constitution

In 1923 the Egyptian lawyers produced a Constitution modelled on that of Belgium. Fuad was now King Fuad, but with limited powers. In April 1923 the British terminated martial law, Saad returned to Egypt, and so did other long-exiled nationalists. The Wafd became a political party with an overwhelming majority in the Chamber of Deputies, and Saad was Prime Minister, but for all the outward appearance of normalizing relationships, secret ultra-nationalist parties remained.

In November 1924 Sir Lee Stack, commander of Egypt's army and governor of the Sudan, was murdered by terrorists. Enraged, Allenby demanded retribution from Saad, prosecution of the assassins, a sum equivalent to $2.5 million, and withdrawal of Egyptian troops from the Sudan. Saad resigned, and King Fuad appointed a new cabinet.

Early years of Independence

In the post-war state of quasi-independence there were three major forces in Egypt. King Fuad, a constitutional monarch, wanted more power than the constitution awarded him, the Wafd party dominated the Chamber of Deputies, and the British still ran almost everything. There were lesser Egyptian political parties and there were large landholders who, although not organized as a party, held substantial powers. As the population grew, there were more landless peasants, but more major landholding landlords (the royal family owned 10% of the land), an overdependence on cotton damaged the economy, and even that was jeopardized by the new artificial fibers, and the dreaded boll-weevil. And education had become its own enemy, a class of young persons had been educated away from the peasantry but there were no "clean hands" jobs for them, and the Depression was on its way.

Anglo-Egyptian Treaty

Egypt found itself uncomfortably situated between Libya and Ethiopia, both occupied by Fascist Italy; although King Fuad supported the Italians, the Wafd did not. But Fuad died in 1936 and was succeeded by his 16 year old son Farouk, and an agreement was reached whereby Britain would continue a 20 year occupation of the Canal Zone, restrict the military to 10,000, and the despised Capitulations would be abolished.

World War II

When the war started there were 60,000 Italians in Egypt, and the Egyptians realized if the British left, the Italians would come. The Italians were altogether too conveniently arranged between Libya and Abyssinia with the highly desirable Nile valley.

The Italians were defeated in North Africa by General Wavell, but then the Germans came in force to support them under the Desert Fox, Rommel, who drove the British back to El Alamein on the Egyptian border. At this point some Egyptians thought they would make an arrangement with the Germans ,and the British distrusted Farouk, so they surrounded his palace with armoured cars and advised him either to abdicate or to form a pro-British government. This repeat of subjection to the British caused unrealistic resentment at the time. After all, if it wasn't going to be the British, it would be the Italians and the Germans.

Surprisingly Egypt prospered during the war, a byproduct of the fact the military needed goods and services. With that there was increased employment, and the entertainment industry in its various forms thrived like never before. In a twist of fate, this time it was the British government that borrowed $2 billion from the Egyptians.

Iraq's Prime Minister suggested a union of the Arab countries in the "Fertile Crescent" and although this did not materialize, an Arab League was formed in 1944.

The First Palestine War

In May 1948 the Arab League went to war with Israel.

On May 14, 1948, the British Mandate officially expired. That same day, the Jewish National Council issued the Declaration of the Establishment of the State of Israel. About 10 minutes later, President Truman officially recognized the State of Israel, and the Soviet Union also quickly recognized Israel.

However, the Palestinians and the Arab League did not recognize the new state, and the very next day, armies from Egypt, Syria, Lebanon and Iraq invaded the former British Mandate to squelch Israel, while Saudi Arabia assisted the Arab armies. Jordan would also get involved in the war, fighting the Israelis around Jerusalem. Initially, the Arab armies numbered over 20,000 soldiers, but the Zionist militia groups like the Lehi, Irgun and Haganah made it possible for Israel to quickly assemble the Israel Defense Forces, still known today simply as the IDF. By the end of 1948, the Israelis had over 60,000 soldiers and the Arab armies numbered over 50,000.

The Israelis began pressing their advantages on both land and air by the fall of 1948, bombing foreign capitals like Damascus while overrunning Arab armies in the British Mandate. In towns like Ramat Rachel and Deir Yassin, close quarter combat in villages led to civilian casualties and charges of massacres. In particular, the Jewish assault on Deir Yassin, which led to the death of about 50 Palestinians, is often labeled a massacre by the Palestinians, although the Israelis asserted that house to house combat made fighting difficult.

Regardless, Palestinians who heard of the news of Jewish attacks on places like Deir Yassin were afraid for their lives and began to flee their homes. At the same time, Palestinians were encouraged by commanders of the Arab armies to clear out of the area until after they could defeat Israel. Palestinians and Jews had been fighting since 1947, and over 250,000 Palestinians had already fled their homes by the time the 1948 War had started. It is unclear how many Palestinians fled from Jewish forces and how many left voluntarily, but by the end of the war over 700,000 Palestinians had fled from their homes in the former British Mandate. Meanwhile, nearly 800,000 Jews had been forcibly expelled from their homes in nations throughout the Middle East, leading to an influx of Jews at the same time Palestinians were leaving.

In late 1948, Israel was on the offensive. That December, the U.N. General Assembly passed Resolution 194, which declared that under a peace agreement, "refugees wishing to return to their homes and live in peace with their neighbors should be permitted to do so," and "compensation should be paid for the property of those choosing not to return." Egypt was so unprepared they used the road maps obtained from an American car dealer, and one of Farouk's mistresses was suborned to pass information to Israel. The Egyptian army was ingloriously routed, 2,000 of its soldiers killed, and Egypt itself was only saved by the British refusing Israeli passage through the Canal Zone, the much-hated by Egypt provision which turned out to be their saviour.

Months later, Israel began signing armistices with Egypt, Jordan, and Syria, which left Israel in control of nearly 75% of the lands that were to be partitioned into the two states under the 1947 plan. Jordan now occupied Judea and Samaria, which later became known as the West Bank due to its position on the western bank of the Jordan River. Jordan also occupied three quarters of Jerusalem, with the Israelis controlling only about a quarter in the western part of the city. To the west, Egypt occupied the Gaza Strip.

The new armistice lines became known as the "Green Line."

Military Rule and Arab Nationalism (1952-1981)

Society of Muslim Brothers

In 1948 the Muslim Brotherhood had 2,000 branches in Egypt and provided education, medical clinics and general welfare for a large element of the poorer classes. The women's auxiliary, Muslim Sisters, and the youth branch, the Rovers (much like Boy Scouts), numbered 40,000. But there was a dark element, the Secret Apparatus, that committed assassinations and bombings. Their "Supreme Guide" was Sheikh Hasan al-Banna, who ordered the assassination of the Prime

Minister; in his turn he was murdered in 1949, presumed to have been killed by government agents. A crackdown ordered by Farouk left 4,000 members of the Brotherhood imprisoned in 1949, but in 1951 an appeal against the group's dissolution was upheld in the courts.

1950 Elections

In the 1950 elections, the Wafd came out ahead with 40% of the vote and set about a program of social reform. School fees were abolished, pensions for widows, orphans and the disabled were created, but plans to distribute land were not fulfilled.

In October 1951, Nahhas leading the Wafd abrogated the 1936 Anglo-Egyptian agreement, declared Farouk was king of both Egypt and the Sudan, and that the British had no further rights in the Canal Zone where Egyptian workers were obliged to go on strike. The Egyptian government immediately dismissed all British employees. In response to these measures, the British retaliated in January 1952 with an attack on the police headquarters in Ismailia, killing 50. Mob violence followed on "Black Saturday" with burning in Cairo of western type hotels and restaurants, including the famed Shepheard's Hotel. 30 people died, hundreds were injured, 400 buildings were destroyed, and the property damage cost $500 million. Eventually the Egyptian army took over, fires were extinguished, and Farouk dismissed the Wafd cabinet. Who was responsible remains unknown. It's probable that it was a spontaneous act that attracted unconnected groups.

Chaos followed, and there were four new governments in six months before Farouk's dismissal.

The Egyptian Officers Cabal

The defeat by Israel was a blow to Egyptian pride, but there were many changes in the Middle East at the time. There had been revolutions in Yemen in 1948, in Syria in 1949, King Abdullah of Jordan was assassinated in 1951, and many secret societies in Egypt plotted to do the same to King Farouk.

At one time a finishing school for the sons of the wealthy, the Egyptian Military Academy had altered its intake of students to those who succeeded in competitive examinations, which brought in a quite different societal group, many from financially modest origins. A "Free Officers Society" was formed, but its origins are disputed and may have initially been multiple groups. Regardless, it was organized along traditional conspiratory lines, in cells of five, and with a hierarchy spreading from each cell.

In 1951 their ethos was to: destroy the British occupation; eliminate feudalism; end the power of capitalism; create social equality; develop a strong people's army; and establish democracy. There was at that time no political party affiliation.

The Free Officers led a revolution in 1952, overthrowing the government on the night of July 22. The CIA, of course, was held responsible, but the actual revolution seems to have been a Keystone Cops affair. Answar Sadat didn't know the timing and had gone to the movies, and Gamal Abdel Nasser's car was stopped by the police because his tail light was not working. The opposition was even less ready, however, and King Farouk was instructed to abdicate. After the U.S. and British declined to help, Farouk willingly gave up power, his infant son was declared successor, and a regency council was installed.

Nasser

The Free Officers found not everyone thought as disinterestedly as they did. Nasser later wrote, "Every man we met sought nothing else but the destruction of another man." The Muslim Brotherhood demanded the Koran should be Egypt's constitution, while textile workers rioted and burnt their factories. In response, the military shot some and executed others.

Democracy was fine as a principle, but in short order the Free Officers concluded it was inefficient and seriously interfered with their views of progress. Parliament was dissolved in December 1952, and in June 1953 the last vestiges of monarchy were abolished. General Muhammad Naguib was elected President, Prime Minister, and Chairman of the Revolutionary Command Council (RCC). Members of the RCC assumed all senior government positions.

Gamal Abdel Nasser

With progressing internal rivalries, the aggressive Nasser came into conflict with Naguib, who resigned from the presidency in February 1954. This delighted Nasser, of course, but the people turned against Nasser and he was forced to ask Naguib to return to office. Nasser then so manipulated affairs that his own supporters took all significant offices, and although Naguib remained as President, he was stripped of any real power.

Possibly in relation to his imperfect demands for British evacuation of Suez, shots were fired at Nasser in Alexandria in 1954. The culprit was found to belong to the Muslim Brotherhood, he and a number of other supposed co-conspirators were executed, and a pogrom on the Brotherhood was initiated. President Naguib was arrested, and the office of President declared void.

Egypt had failed against Israel in the earlier war, and Israel continued to retaliate against incursions from Gaza, which was still Egyptian held. In one case, there was a bizarre, fortunately frustrated, affair in which Mossad agents planned to blow up American institutions in Cairo to damage US/Egyptian relations. Nasser wanted to equip his army to hold off Israel, but the British and Americans were not interested in helping him. In his turn he was not interested in joining the Baghdad Pact, effectively NATO for the Middle East, which he construed as in America's interests against Russia but did nothing for Egypt's concerns with Israel.

Thus, when Nasser attended a conference of "non-aligned" nations, he was ripe for the communist picking, and in September 1955 an agreement was made with Czechoslovakia (a Soviet satellite) for a $200 million worth of arms, to be bought with cotton.

Aswan High Dam

Dating back to the first years of the 20th century, Britain had helped to improve the Nile Valley irrigation, extensively increasing the available arable land. One such project, opened in 1902, was the Aswan Dam, which had been elevated in height twice since its first formation. Plans to put dams on the White Nile would have left Egypt at the mercy of Sudan, and they were discounted even though they were sound from an engineering viewpoint. The ultimate decision was to make a new and even higher dam at Aswan, from which year round irrigation of an additional million acres, and huge electrical resources, were anticipated. The drawback was the billion dollars it would cost.

The World Bank offered to fund the first phase, partly supported by the U.S. and the U.K., but both countries attached strings – control over Egypt's economy, no arms deals, and no contracts with communist countries. In June 1956 the Soviets offered Nasser $1,120,000,000 at 2% interest for the construction of the dam. Egypt hesitantly agreed to the conditions imposed effectively by the U.S., but the day after their consent was obtained, John Foster Dulles, U.S. Secretary of State, cancelled the American offer. Nasser felt they'd made a fool of him.

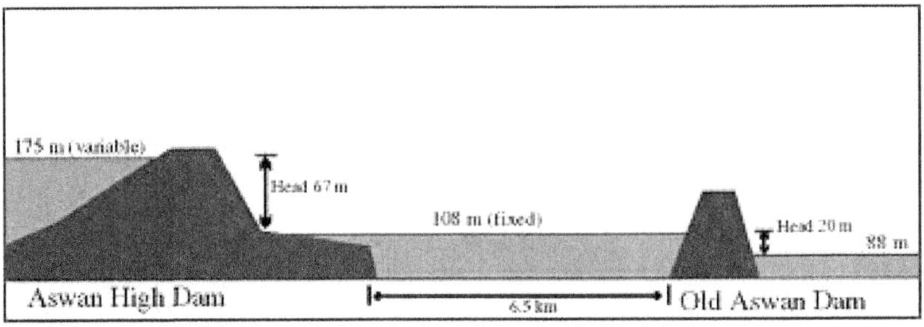

In direct response, in July 1956 Nasser invaded and occupied the Suez Canal Zone, announced the Canal was to be nationalized, and the tolls charged would be used to pay for the Aswan High Dam. Not generally recognized by the world, the Canal did in fact belong to Egypt. Although there were shareholders for the seized property, appropriate compensation was offered. The British were convinced the Egyptians were incapable of running the affairs of the Canal, but the Egyptians proved them wrong.

Britain and France, together with Israel, set up an invasion force, but the lack of support from President Eisenhower and the opposition of the Commonwealth nations deterred them and the invasion was called off. Egypt was left in charge of her own Canal, and Nasser was the hero of the day. There followed an ugly period of expulsion of French, British and Israeli citizens and companies from Egypt.

Meanwhile the government of Egypt underwent radical changes. With a new constitution women were given the vote, political parties were banned, and there was to be one voice only, the National Union.

In 1958 the Soviet Union provided funding for the Aswan High Dam project.

Arab Nationalism

After the Suez Canal War, Egyptian leader Gamal Abdel Nasser envisioned creating a unified Arab world, commonly referred to as pan-Arabism. Nasser was the consummate pan-Arab leader in the 1960s, positioning himself as the leader of the Arab world through increasing incitement against Israel with rhetoric. Most Egyptians thought of themselves as Egyptians and only Egyptians, but Nasser concluded there was a potential for group strength by his declaration that Egypt was a member of the Arab nations. From this sprang a short lived union with Syria, to form the United Arab Republic (UAR), in which Syria very much played second fiddle and eventually withdrew in September 1961.

For a time a spirit of "pan-Arabism" was popular, but this movement, nebulous in itself, was redefined as Arab socialism and widely interpreted as state ownership of land and property, not unlike Mehmet Ali's control of Egypt. Pan-Arabism would also take another blow during the Six Day War.

June 1967 war

Israel found itself in possession of more land after 1948 than envisioned by the U.N. Partition Plan, but the Green Line still left it less than 10 miles wide in some positions. In the summer of 1967, the armies of Jordan and Syria mobilized near Israel's borders, while Egypt's army mobilized in the Sinai Peninsula just west of the Gaza Strip. Combined, the Arab armies numbered over 200,000 soldiers.

In early June 1967, the Israelis captured Jordanian intelligence that indicated an invasion was imminent. When Nasser declared an embargo to shipping through the Tiran Straits at the opening to the Gulf of Aqaba. Israel responded on June 5 by a pre-emptive air strike against the Egyptian planes on the ground and destroyed 80% of the Egyptian Air Force. In three days the Israeli army took the Sinai peninsula and 5000 Egyptian soldiers were prisoner, 20,000 died mostly from neglect by their officers, some of battle wounds. On June 8, the Israeli army halted at the east bank of the Gulf of Suez. The Suez Canal was closed.

Over the course of a war lasting less than a week, the Israelis had overwhelmed the Egyptians in the west, destroying thousands of tanks and capturing the Gaza Strip and the entire Sinai Peninsula. At the same time, Israel drove the Jordanians out of Jerusalem and the West Bank, and it captured the Golan Heights from Syria near the border of Lebanon. Israel had tripled the size of the lands it controlled and had gone from less than 10 miles wide in some spots to over 200 miles wide from the Sinai Peninsula to the West Bank. Israel also unified Jerusalem.

As with the 1948 war, the 1967 war ended with an armistice, creating war heroes out of Yitzhak Rabin and Ariel Sharon. Nasser in shame resigned his posts, but the people of Egypt begged him to reconsider, and he returned to office.

The hand of the USSR was also strengthened as the Arab states now found themselves more reliant on the Soviets for arms. The policy of "3 No's" developed – *no negotiation; no recognition; no peace with Israel.* There followed prolonged skirmishing at sea and in the air over the Suez Canal and adjacent Egyptian air space, called the "War of Attrition."

Nasser died unexpectedly in September 1970, bringing Sadat to power.

Anwar Sadat

Anwar Sadat was Vice-President and the logical successor to Nasser, but he was not highly regarded despite being voted into that position. Unexpectedly he proved himself more forthright than expected and fired Nasser's former associates, gaining popularity when he discharged Nasser's secret agents and made a bonfire of the secret information they had amassed.

Initially, Sadat continued Nasser's policy of friendship with the USSR, and Egypt continued to receive military supplies from them. Eventually, however, Sadat came to resent the domineering attitude of the Soviets and their continuing control of some of the armaments supplied to him.

October (Yom Kippur) War

On October 6, 1973, Syria and Egypt caught Israel off guard during the Jewish holy holiday of Yom Kippur, surprise attacking the Sinai Peninsula and Golan Heights. Although they initially made gains, the Israelis turned the tide within a week, going on the counteroffensive and winning the war within 3 weeks. The Israelis crossed the Suez Canal and were within an hour's drive of Cairo when a cease-fire was agreed, leaving Israel soldiers on the Egyptian side of the canal, and Egyptian soldiers, surrounded by Israelis, in the Sinai.

The Yom Kippur War was the last concerted invasion of Israel by conventional Arab armies, but it underscored how entangled the West and the Soviet Union had gotten in the region. The British and French had been allied with Israel in the 1950s, including during the Suez Canal War, and the United States assisted Israel by providing weapons as early as the 1960s. As a way of counteracting Western influence, the Soviets developed ties with the Arab nations.

For Egypt, the military benefit was a minus, but the psychological benefit inadvertently proved enormous. After years tolerating an Israeli occupation of the Sinai, and effective blockage of the Suez Canal, the Arab oil producing countries said they would progressively reduce output by 5%

a month, and an embargo on the U.S. until Israel withdrew. Iran followed suit by raising prices. Eventually, after much shuttle diplomacy by U.S. Secretary of State Henry Kissinger, an agreement was reached by which the Israelis withdrew to 10 miles east of the Canal.

The limited success achieved in forcing Israeli withdrawal, attributed by the Egyptians to Sadat, caused a boom in building along the Canal, opportunities for investment in Egypt, a swing away from socialist government control in the direction of free enterprise, and tentative easing of relations with the US. For a number of reasons, including some just listed, the USSR reduced and then cancelled military aid.

However, increasing wealth and job opportunities in other Arab states resulted in a significant outflowing of Egyptian labor and professional talent, bringing on debt that once again led to more than half the state's incomes going to repayments. At the suggestion of the IMF, subsidies to food and fuel were reduced with significant rise in prices, particularly in regard to bread since Egypt was importing half of what it consumed.

The Camp David Accords - Peace with Israel

Sadat undertook an almost unbelievable mission. Addressing the People's Assembly in November 1977, he made what was probably a rhetorical claim: he was prepared to go to the Knesset in Jerusalem to seek peace. Walter Cronkite asked if he meant it, and Sadat said he did. Cronkite asked Prime Minister Begin of Israel if he would accept such a visit, and he said he would.

Sadat flew to Israel, was received with every courtesy, addressed the Knesset and flew back to Egypt to a great welcome. To everyone's surprise Begin came to Egypt on Christmas Day when he met with President Carter and Sadat. After the Yom Kippur War, President Carter's administration sought to establish a peace process that would settle the conflict in the Middle East, while also reducing Soviet influence in the region. On September 17, 1978, after secret negotiations at the presidential retreat Camp David, Egyptian President Anwar Sadat and Israeli Prime Minister Menachem Begin signed a peace treaty between the two nations, in which Israel ceded the Sinai Peninsula to Egypt in exchange for a normalization of relations, making Egypt the first Arab adversary to officially recognize Israel. Carter also tried to create a peace process that would settle the rest of the conflict vis-à-vis the Israelis and Palestinians, but it never got off the ground.

For the Camp David Accords, Begin and Sadat won the Nobel Peace Prize, but the peace treaty, did not raise Egypt's popularity with other Arab states, noticeably not with the Palestinians.

Begin, Carter and Sadat at the signing ceremony

Naturally, the peace treaty and the negotiations that led up to it brought Egypt closer to the US side of the Cold War, and the U.S. began supplying arms and aid to Egypt. This aid was not in large enough quantities to endanger Israel, but enough that the Egyptian military could enjoy the pleasure of playing with their military hardware. Tourism, a vital industry for Egypt, was also revived.

However, the negative aspect to life came from increasing numbers of young persons with education but no work available to their level of learning. And inevitably this breeds discontent. There developed increasing numbers of secret societies with fundamental Islamism as their tenets, in parallel with changes occurring in Iran. Leaders were captured and often imprisoned if not executed, and Islamic forms of dress, previously uncommon, were adopted. Beards were grown, attempts were made in the universities to separate the sexes, and plots were hatched to kill Sadat. Increasingly, suppression became the order of the day.

Since 1977, party politics had been restored, the Wafd party returned, and the Muslim Brotherhood was permitted to have representatives as individuals but not as a party since religion was banned as a political party issue. Still, only the National Democratic Party was of consequence.

The peace treaty with Israel eventually cost Sadat his life. At a military parade, October 6, 1981, Sadat was in the stands taking the salute. A young officer jumped out of a truck, surprising those in the stands totally unaware of his intentions, and he began shooting at Sadat with an AK-47. The military officers responsible for the assassination had ties to the opposition group Muslim Brotherhood, as well as Ayman al-Zawahiri, who later became one of the senior leaders of al-Qaeda and the new head upon Osama bin Laden's death.

The Hosni Mubarak Years

The day after Sadat's murder, the Assembly appointed the Vice President, General Hosni Mubarak to succeed to the President's post, as the fourth in that role in Egypt. He had previously served in the Air Force, was highly regarded as an administrator, had been Vice President since 1975, and had been sent on a number of diplomatic missions to Heads of State representing Sadat. Mubarak was among those wounded when Sadat was killed.

Mubarak entered into his tasks in a quiet way, first improving social conditions with an increase in low cost housing and state subsidised production of clothing, furniture, and medicine. He walked a fine line, trying to keep the friendship and financial support of both the USSR and the U.S., as well as the difficulty of placating Israel without offending the Palestinians and the Arab powers.

Many of the strictures imposed by Sadat were removed and political prisoners were released. He did, however, crack down on Islamists, particularly the Muslim Brotherhood, and many were jailed. The previously tolerated outward signs were banned, including beards, galabias (male gowns) and female head scarves on university campuses.

1984 USSR and USA

Relationships with the USSR were improved, and the terms for repayment of debt were eased; ambassadors were exchanged after 1984. The US continued to support Egypt financially, between one and three billion dollars a year, represented by arms, capital goods and food, and some capital improvements in substructures as well as social assistance.

1985 Achille Lauro

On October 7, 1985, four Palestinian terrorists hijacked the Achille Lauro liner off Egypt and threw a handicapped Leon Klinghoffer (an American Jew) overboard. They were refused permission to dock in Syria, but after negotiations they were permitted to dock in Port Said, and after two days of negotiations, the Egyptian government compromised with an offer of immunity to the Palestinians who were to be flown to Tunisia aboard an Egyptian commercial airliner. President Reagan, however, ordered U.S. fighter planes to force the Egyptian civilian plane to land at a NATO base in Italy.

On October 10th there was a stand-off between the Italian Carabinieri and U.S. Special Forces, including SEAL Team 6. The Carabinieri prevailed, but diplomatic relations between Italy and the US were severely strained, as they were with Egypt, for which the U.S. had rather less concern.

1989 Arab League membership restored

The other Arab states gradually came to accept Egypt's working relations with Israel, and without much said, their own relations with Egypt were restored. Egypt was the only state to have had its membership suspended in the Arab League, but in 1989 Egypt was restored to its prior position and the offices of the League returned to Cairo.

1991 Gulf War

Mubarak lent his services to ameliorate the tense relations between Saddam Hussein's Iraq and

Kuwait in an effort to prevent the invasion, then to try to stop the invasion. Finally he provided 40,000 Egyptian soldiers to drive Saddam out of Kuwait during Operation Desert Storm. The Egyptian infantry were among the first in Saudi Arabia, and their lead encouraged support from other Arab nations.

2003 Iraq War

President Mubarak argued against the invasion of Iraq, believing the issue the Arabs had with Israel was of greater priority. Mubarak also asserted that destroying one bin Laden would only produce a hundred more. Once the die was cast, though, he did not advocate an immediate pull-out of U.S. forces, knowing chaos would ensue. Furthermore, there was nothing to be gained by criticizing the Americans too harshly when receiving so much aid from them.

2005 Election

Mubarak was re-elected by majority votes of Assembly in 1987, 1993, and 1999. In the 2005 election it was determined the President would be chosen by popular vote, as in the U.S. Naturally, there were substantiated complaints of vote rigging and corruption, and when one of the rival candidates, dissident Ayman Nour, had the temerity to complain, he was convicted of forgery and sentenced to five years.

Assassination attempts

At least six attempts were made to kill Mubarak after he was made President, mostly involving various extremist Islamic groups. In turn, those groups were severely suppressed, to the extent that as many as 20,000 persons were probably incarcerated, and there was no question that police standards failed to meet the requirements of a civilized society. However, it was found in 2005 that 72 of the elected deputies, who stood as individuals, were in fact Muslim Brotherhood members, a sign of the reach of Egypt's largest and most organized opposition group.

An Emergency Law dating to 1967 gave the police, who were directed by the army and the ruling clique of generals, virtually unrestrained powers. In effect, there were no civil rights and anyone could be (and often were) imprisoned without explanation. Numbers are indefinite but there may have been 30,000 persons held in this manner in Mubarak's police state.

The military undoubtedly believed it when they said such measures were necessary to control Islamic extremism, including the Muslim Brotherhood.

State corruption during Mubarak's presidency:

Police states always seem to foster corruption, resulting in rules that are impossible to observe and payments made to petty officials to evade punishment for them.

On a larger scale, absolute power corrupts absolutely. At his trial it was alleged Mubarak had money tucked away in the amount of many billions of dollars.

Muslim Brotherhood

The Muslim Brotherhood was a thorn in the side of Egypt's secular rulers for generations, and now they stand on the precipice of power in Egypt with Mubarak's removal. Naturally, that means more attention than ever is being paid to them.

The Muslim Brotherhood bases its beliefs on its own interpretation of the Koran, and not unlike fundamental Christians who can find whatever they please in the Bible, fundamental Islamists can find whatever they please in the Koran.

The Brotherhood was started as a movement in 1928 by Hassan al-Banna with the excellently expressed intentions of coupling the teaching of Islam with the practice of good deeds – not unlike mendicant friars and the better monasteries of the Christian Middle Ages. But good intentions were not enough, and political involvement followed. If you believed the problems of the poor were because the British wanted them that way, what was more logical than to oppose the British? And if the British were driven out, why not all infidels? The drive became to establish that "Islam is the solution," and the law would be the Sharia.

The Brotherhood flourished in the early and mid-20th century by providing much needed social services, schools, sports and medical facilities, and in 20 years it had grown to a membership of 2 million. But al-Banna, who was assassinated in 1948, saw fit to form a paramilitary force, called "Special Apparatus," and he used them in "terrorist" actions against the British and the Jews, but also against leading Egyptians such as the Prime Minister.

In 1948, while the British were still in Egypt, the Muslem Brotherhood was banned. In 1952, when the Free Officers had their own revolution, the Muslim Brotherhood came into favor again, since they had all worked in the "underground" together. There followed an on-again off-again relationship with government. The Brotherhood (aka the Ikhwan) were popular and numerically powerful; they had a component that wished to serve the needy, but they also had "activists" who thought killing the opposition was the way to go, and promoted *jihad* (struggle) as the preferable way of life.

Thus, periodically the Brotherhood was part of the mainstream political system, as in 1984 when they allied with the Wafd party, 1987 when they allied with Labor and Liberal parties, and in 2000 they held 17 seats in the Assembly. But Mubarak was concerned with the rise in legitimate representation of the party he feared, and a law was passed proscribing any party with religious affiliation. With that, many members of the Brotherhood were arrested, effectively for no better reason than their membership in the party.

The Arab Spring

Tunisia seemed like a weird place for the removal of Mubarak to have its origins. In Sidi Bouzid, a small central Tunisian town of no consequence, there was a 26 years old barrow boy who was no more important than his town, but whose name will now linger in the history books. Mohamed Bouazizi's father was dead and Mohamed was the sole support of his family of eight. He had for seven years made their living by selling vegetables from a handcart and stall.

Although he should have been licensed, licences were not obtainable and periodically he paid off the corrupt police to the cost of five dollars, a day's wages. From what he earned he kept his family fed and his sisters in school. But on December 17, 2010, a female police officer not only confiscated his cart and produce but also insulted the memory of his deceased father. Although one might have expected Mohamed to know better, he went to the office of the local authorities to complain about his treatment and the inability to get properly licensed, which led to recurring harassment. The female office worker refused him permission to talk to anyone in authority and slapped him for daring to complain. One can only speculate on how he felt or why he did it, but Mohamed doused himself in gasoline, and set fire to himself outside the gates of the building in which he had been so insulted.

Mohamed was taken first to the local hospital which was not equipped to deal with injuries such as his, so he was driven 70 miles to the city of Sfax where he was treated. Because his self-immolation was gaining notoriety, he was transferred to a hospital near Tunis where he was visited by President Ben Ali. Mohamed lived in agony for two weeks, then died on January 4, 2011. During the two weeks he lingered, there was increasing unrest in Tunisia. Disturbances were not unknown, but they were not everyday events, and they were usually suppressed without bloodshed. Freedom to express an opinion was, however, very definitely not part of Tunisian life. Lahseen Naji had suffered death by accidental electrocution on December 22nd when he climbed a power tower during a demonstration, and on the 24th Mohamed Ammari was shot dead by police in one of several demonstrations across Tunisia. On 14th January, 2011, President Zine al-Abidine Ben Ali of Tunisia and his family left the country, reportedly taking a plane load of gold with them.

Though he certainly could not have intended it, Mohammed Bouazizi quite unconsciously set off what became designated as the "Arab Spring." It came about gradually but mounted and mounted until it could not be denied. Mohamed Bouazizi died in Tunis on January 4th 2011, but in the three weeks that passed between the times of his self-injury and his death, the world had been apprised of the issues and the internet was abuzz with gossip. Hand held communications characterized these revolutions like never before – Twitter and Facebook were sovereign – although they had been known to be used in coordinating mob activities in the "protests" in western cities such as London and Toronto.

It was expected that the protests in Tunisia would spread to other countries, and Mohamed ElBaradei, known to the West for his activities in nuclear weapons inspections, had prophetically forecasted they would appear in his own country, Egypt. And they did – much of it played out before the well placed television cameras with continuous "real time" coverage of the action in Tahrir Square and the long bridge over the River Nile.

The movement in Egypt took hold on January 25th 2011 with what was known to them as The Day of Revolt. Although it was Cairo that was seen on the western TV, there were protests against President Hosni Mubarak all over the country. To some extent they faced off with the police, on the whole they were non-violent. But in the next two days it began to get ugly, stones were thrown, shots were fired, a few hundred were injured and a very small number killed; barbed wire went up and corrugated iron sheets were used by the most aggressive of the protestors.

Tahrir Square in Cairo is a large open area, adjacent to one of the several bridges over the Nile. It must have been supposed by the authorities that they would disperse and go about their business, but day by day the crowds grew, they did not disperse, and they called for the government to fall. Some said they would remain in the Square until President Mubarak resigned.

Friday after the believers leave the mosques is the traditional time for mob action in the Muslim world. On 28th January, which they termed Friday of Rage, the authorities had pre-emptively closed down communication devices, but the protestors in thousands gathered in public spaces such as Tahrir Square. The army, in general more sympathetic with the people, was called in to reinforce the police numbers. It was a very big, but a relatively non-hostile gathering which continued in the demand Mubarak should go. Progressively as numbers increased, so did the feelings of hostility, and there were threatening displays of military might.

Tahrir Square in February 2011

President Mubarak discharged his entire cabinet, and although on TV he sympathised with the demands of the protestors, he also defended the attempt to suppress the protest. President Obama called President Mubarak, and advised him to "give meaning" to promises to improve the lot of the people of Egypt.

On 29th January, President Mubarak appointed his intelligence chief, Omar Suleiman, as Vice President, and the Air Minister, Ahmed Shafiq, as Prime Minister, confirming there was no intention of the military to relinquish control of government. They would only change the seating. The crowds became less satisfied, overt fighting occurred with the police and to a lesser extent the army, and there was now reported a total of 74 deaths.

The last day of January was given a slogan type name even before the event: The March of the Millions. How many came to Tahrir Square was impossible to tell since capacity was a quarter of that, but the TV certainly showed it packed. Mubarak promised to cut short his Presidency, but the crowd was not satisfied and predictably the mood became ugly on both sides. That same day, the army (which had always been considered a "people's army") declared the people had legitimate rights and they would not use force against them.

As unrest mounted, February 2nd became the Battle of the Camel, and television viewers were treated to a bizarre scene of men mounted on horses and camels riding aggressively into the mob, inciting further violence. The crowds got more assertive, less holiday-like, and destructive forces came into play. The headquarters of the governing NDP party was torched and other government offices were invaded. 26 deaths were reported.

As February unrolled, the crowds increased, noticeably in Tahrir Square, but also elsewhere in Egypt; "march of a million" became a popular slogan. The competence of many Egyptians to express themselves lucidly in English facilitated TV interviews. And President Mubarak announced his term of office would constitutionally cease in September 2011 and would not seek re-election. Obviously Mubarak did not understand the "mood of the mob," which wanted him out of office in minutes, not months. Following on the President's directions, the Army told the people their message had been heard and they should now go home, but they didn't. And it began, inevitably, to grow more violent, with the throwing of Molotov cocktails and armoured personnel carriers very visible as a threat on the Square.

There followed a week of uncertainty, government resignations that didn't happen, and unheeded demands for Mubarak to go. Then, on 11th February, nearly three weeks after the protests began, Vice-President Omar Suleiman announced the resignation of President Mubarak, with immediate effect. Joy in Tahrir Square was unbridled. Mubarak let it be known he would not leave Egypt, and it was found he and his family had gone to Sharm el-Sheikh on the Red Sea. Power, however, continued to rest with the generals, and on further analysis it was unclear what had been achieved.

Further career of Hosni Mubarak

At the end of February, the courts issued an unnecessary order prohibiting Mubarak from leaving Egypt and placing him under house arrest in a palace. In April the courts announced he was to be questioned for charges of corruption and abuse of power, and in May the charges were escalated to premeditated murder of the Tahrir Square protestors. By this time it was evident Mubarak's health was fading, always with the *caveat* that health issues are commonly used to escape legal retribution.

At the end of May he was found, *in absentia*, guilty of the nebulous charge of shutting down communication via the internet and fined $35 million.

In August, Mubarak was brought to court on a stretcher and held in a cage while the trial proceeded with charges of murder, for which Egypt still exacts the death penalty. He was ordered held in a military hospital while court proceedings unfolded, which they did very gradually, perhaps too slowly.

What had started as a show trial concluded without TV coverage and reached rather peculiar conclusions. Mubarak was found not guilty of ordering the actions to control the protest, but guilty of failing to stop it when it had started. The penalty was to be life imprisonment.

Mubarak and his family were absolved of all charges relating to finance, despite rumors they had skimmed up to $70 billion from public funds.

All police who were charged with Mubarak in relation to deaths of protestors were found not guilty by virtue of insufficient evidence. Unsurprisingly the crowds were not satisfied.

Omar Suleiman

Suleiman was appointed Vice President by President Hosni Mubarak on 29 January 2011. Undoubtedly Mubarak had good reasons in his own mind for this choice, but since Suleiman was Head of Intelligence, and Intelligence had an extremely unsavory reputation for torture (some in association with the CIA rendition program), he was obviously not going to be the people's choice.

On 11 February 2011, it was given to Suleiman to announce Mubarak's resignation. However, he did not move into the position of President, as that power was transferred to the Armed Forces Supreme Council.

Suleiman withdrew altogether from politics and on 19 July 2012 died in a United States hospital.

2012 Election

There were two candidates of note, and with the expectation of biased polling it was expected Ahmed Shafiq, the former chief of the air force and prime minister under President Hosni Mubarak, would be the clear victor.

The Muslim Brotherhood openly ran their candidate, Khairat al-Shater, a millionaire businessman and deputy leader of the Brotherhood. It was thought he might be disqualified and prevented from running, which in fact was the case. Mohammed Mursi was originally the reserve candidate for the Muslim Brotherhood, and he did not put in his nomination papers until the very last day. After al-Shater was declared ineligible, the Brotherhood undertook to support Mohammed Mursi.

Unsurprisingly, he was one of the two candidates at the peak of counting, taking 24% of vote in the first round in May, and thus he was one of the two in the constitutionally provided run off. In the run-off, the vote was declared to have been 51.73% in Mursi's favor, and he was to be the 5th President of Egypt. Thus, on June 30, 2012, Mohammed Mursi was sworn in as the first ever democratically elected President of Egypt.

Mursi is a 60-year-old engineer who studied at Cairo University in the 1970s, then in the United States took further studies for his PhD at the University of Southern California. He was also an Assistant Professor at California State University from 1982 to 1985. Two of his children were born in the U.S. and are therefore citizens there. When he returned to Egypt he was made head of the engineering department at Zagazig University.

Mursi, like many professionals, associated himself with the Muslim Brotherhood. When they were not allowed membership as a party, he served as an independent in the Assembly from 2000 to 2005, when he lost his seat in what may have been an unfair electoral process.

The Brotherhood chose him as their spokesperson, and after Hosni Mubarak resigned he was appointed chairman of the Freedom and Justice Party, which won the majority of seats in both the upper and lower houses of Assembly.

There is always fear of extremist Islamism associated with the Brotherhood, and Mursi has said he will institute the Brotherhood's slogan, "Islam is the solution." At the same time, he has claimed he has plans for moderation. Whether the two are compatible remains to be seen, but he has rejected any idea he would turn Egypt into a theocracy. He has said he looks for a new constitution to protect civil rights, but at the same time follow the tenets of Islamic law.

Hisham Qandil

Egypt's President Mohammed Mursi has asked Hisham Qandil, the minister of water resources in the current government, to become the country's youngest prime minister since Gamal Abdul Nasser in 1954. He is not from the Muslim Brotherhood, but as a rival politician has explained, Mursi "brought in someone who is not from the Brotherhood, but whose ideology is similar."

It is not clear how much power Mr Qandil will have. A decree issued in June gave the Supreme Council of the Armed Forces all legislative power and veto power on matters relating to national security, while the president will have final say on key appointments and policies. In point of fact, despite the dramatic changes since Tahrir Square, the generals are still running Egypt.

Qandil has a background similar to Mursi. He is a graduate in engineering from Cairo University, has a PhD from North Carolina, and has been a bureaucrat at the ministry of water resources and irrigation's National Water Research Centre (NWRC), a matter of vital interest in Egypt. He has said his will be a government of technocrats who will have professional competence and will not tolerate corruption.

However, the choice of members for his cabinet does not altogether bear out his words, and the generals remain. Of the 18 ministers named, two are members of the Muslim Brotherhood's Freedom and Justice Party (FJP). Major-Gen Ahmed Jamal al-Din will be interior minister, Foreign Minister Mohammed Kamal Amr and Finance Minister Mumtaz al-Said will keep their posts; Field Marshal Mohammed Hussein Tantawi, the head of the ruling Supreme Council of the Armed Forces (Scaf), will be defence minister; Mustafa Musaad will be education minister; Tariq Wafiq, head of the FJP's housing committee, will be housing minister; the minister of religious endowments will be Osama al-Abd, the president of al-Azhar University.

Egypt has changed, but how much remains to be seen. The new President is a member of an Islamist party that has been known for both its social values and its tendency to assassinate. The new Prime Minister has been chosen in the President's image. And yet real power still remains with the generals, and it is highly questionable whether any fundamental changes have occurred.

Printed in Great Britain
by Amazon

39344085R00069